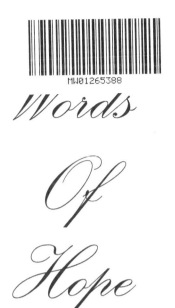

Words

Of

Hope

Help for the hurting heart

Joyce L. Powell

WORDS OF HOPE

Published by A Place of Grace Publishing, 656 Deer Run Pass, Canyon Lake, TX 78133

ISBN: 10: 1517313449
ISBN-13: 978-1517313449

To my father, mother, brother, and sister. Each of you enriched my life and helped make me who I am today. I miss you all terribly but cling to the Hope of Heaven where, in hope, I stand confident we shall meet again. I will look for you at the feet of Jesus.

INTRODUCTION

Words of hope breathed life into my heart when death reigned in the hidden place where nobody sees!

Expecting God to do His work, my confidence and trust in Him, and the anticipation of the breakthrough out of the darkness and into the light kept my soul hanging on when my spirit wanted to let go. Shakespeare wrote about hope when he said, "Eating the air on promise of supply." That is where I lived for a time.

When the unobtainable, impossible, irrevocable brought darkness and despondency, hope raised me from the pit; breath by breath—step by step— moment by moment until desperate, miserable despair gradually, slowly, steadily became optimism, anticipation, and confidence to remember to have faith, trust, and to believe my God.

During my long days of depression after the death of my baby sister, I wanted only to be left alone. Satan likes to isolate us, to make us think nobody understands. But God would not leave me alone, using my precious husband, family and friends to encourage me through my grief.

This book was birthed from that experience as God encouraged me to encourage others during times of anxiety, grief, depression, and the general harshness of the world in which we wander until we rest at home with Him.

Please, make this book personal. I have left lots of white space in which you may write, scribble, jot, and notate what God speaks as you read. Dive into His Word. Seek Him. You will find Him honest, true, faithful, steadfast, compassionate, and much more as He waits for you with open arms. Trust Him. I promise you will never regret it.

Also scattered throughout the pages are precious honest testimonies from ladies who have struggled, and some continue to struggle, with depression, anxiety, grief, loss, physical pain... I know their stories will touch your heart and leave you changed. Some names have been changed for personal privacy. The testimonies are written by each woman. I wanted you to hear their hearts in their voice, not mine. I know God will bless you as you read each one.

I have prayed over, wept over, lost sleep over the writing of this book like none other I have written. If you are reading this, I have prayed for you—many times. I pray you find hope and encouragement from our Lord as you turn the pages.

In His Grace…

Special thanks to the women who so honestly shared
their own struggles in order that you might be
encouraged in the Lord. I am grateful beyond anything
I am able to express.

Angie, Ina, Jeanne, Lisa, Marie,
Melanie, Patricia, Wanda

And as always, I am more than grateful to my sweet
man for putting up with clean laundry piled on the
freezer, nights of pizza when he would rather have had
steak, times he waited for days for me to buy
groceries... Thank you. I love you, more!

Chapter One

Refreshing Hope

O God, you are my God,

earnestly I seek you;

my soul thirsts

for you,

my body longs

for you,

in a dry and weary land

where there is no water.

Psalm 63:1

Living in South Texas I am familiar with months of hot dry weather and landscape that is weary from the lack of refreshing rain. During long hot summers, local meteorologists may predict a slight chance of rain, raising the hope of cattle ranchers, farmers, and citizens who long for the dust to be washed from the trees. However, forecast and reality often collide leaving nothing but dashed hope and continued longing for refreshing. In years of true drought, prayers for rain rise up.

Life has taught me that my soul can also experience drought; times when the busyness of *doing* for God interferes with my *being* with God. When that happens, it is not long before my soul feels barren and dry, and I begin to wonder why God seems distant. Have you had that experience? If I am not careful, I will then begin to live in past journeys with God and past victories for God— only remembering when.

Then it happens! A loving, merciful, gracious God reminds me He is near; watching, waiting, calling me back to the throne room; drawing me back to His Word where He reminds me that during the barren dry times of life, my soul thirsts for Him, and His love is better than life. He encourages me to remember He is my help and the reason I sing, and He cleanses my heart with His springs of living water.

Are you in the midst of spiritual drought? I have good news. There is refreshing hope waiting for you in the presence of the Father. No fancy words required. A humble heart will do.

Hope for Daily Living

Have you ever walked through a spiritual drought? If so, describe the circumstances.

Read Psalm 143. When David was in the midst of hopelessness and depression, he prayed asking God in His faithfulness to hear David's cry for mercy and come to David's relief. What else did David say to God?

According to verse 10, what was David's ultimate request of God? Are you willing to completely surrender your will to God? If you are not sure, take the time to settle that now.

Read James 1:5. How do you see this verse in relationship to giving you hope in the midst of personal trials, spiritual dry seasons, or grief and loss?

Heavenly Father, today I pray for wisdom to earnestly seek You, to believe You, to trust You, and I ask You to safeguard my heart against any doubt the enemy might attempt to use against me. I thank You for the hope I have through Jesus Christ Your Only Begotten Son. Help me, please, as I surrender my will to Yours. In the Name of Jesus. Amen

Chapter two

Courage to Hope

Have I not commanded you?

Be strong and courageous.

Do   not be terrified;

do not be discouraged,

for the LORD

your God will be with you

wherever you go.

Joshua 1:9

Do you have the courage to hope? Job did. In Job 13:15 we read his words, "Though he slay me, yet will I hope in him…" King David did. In Psalm 25:5 we read his words, "…my hope is in you all day long." The prophet Micah did. In Micah 7:7 we read his words, "But as for me, I watch in hope for the LORD…"

What is hope? Strong's Concordance defines hope as "to wait expectantly." Webster's dictionary defines hope as "desire accompanied by expectation of or belief in fulfillment." I define hope as expectantly waiting on God to act on my behalf.

It takes courage to hope. After the death of Moses, God told Joshua, "You and all these people get ready to cross the Jordan River…" Joshua's instant promotion from the position of aide to the role of leader probably caused him to shake in his sandals. But God's promise in Joshua 1:9 must have given Joshua the courage to hope; "for the LORD your God will be with you wherever you go."

Are you discouraged as you wait for answers to life's situations? Is there something you need? Healing. Provision. Reconciliation. Take courage in the LORD as you wait on God to act

on your behalf. Remember His words to
Joshua, "for the LORD your God will be with
you wherever you go." God is your courage to
hope!

Hope for Daily Living

Have you ever needed courage to hope? If so,
describe the circumstances.

Read Nehemiah 1. When Nehemiah's heart was
crushed over the condition of his beloved
Jerusalem, broken down walls and gates
burned with fire, he wept before the LORD for
the courage to approach King Artaxerxes and
ask for help in rebuilding the city. What did
Nehemiah ask of God? Make a list.

Nehemiah found courage to hope in the midst of fear. Read verse two and three again. Ask God to help you pray through your fear and commit to say **yes** to God in spite of your circumstances. Write your commitment below.

Heavenly Father, today I pray for the courage to seek you for my needs and trust you for the results. Give me the courage to admit my fear yet step boldly into your will. Remind me that when You place something on my heart to accomplish, You have already made the way. I thank you for giving me the courage to hope. In the precious Name of Jesus. Amen.

Chapter three

Hang Onto Hope

But the needy
will not
always be forgotten,
nor the hope
of the
afflicted
ever perish.

Psalm 9:18

Fierce thunderstorms, floods, and tornadoes have recently ravaged portions of our nation. Uprooted trees and air-born roofs appear as minor inconveniences when compared to those whose lives have been snuffed out by the power of the unrelenting wind and rain. In the aftermath, a deluge of news reports described the helplessness and hopelessness felt by the loved ones of those sacrificed to the tempest.

Locally our spiritual, emotional, and physical resources were tested as a forty foot wall of water raced down the Blanco River under cover of night and washed away homes as families slept; helpless against the powerful assault of the raging water.

How do we reconcile the hope promised in God's Word with the cruelty of life's circumstances? How does a father who loses the struggle to save his wife and two children from the raging floodwaters wait patiently or have an expectation for his future? How does a young couple beginning their family look forward in hope-filled anticipation after all their belongings are washed away? When we face the reality of life's worst, how do we believe for God's best?

When we feel we are going to perish, when our heart has been destroyed, or when we have lost courage, how do we hang onto hope?

Seek God. Trust God. Believe God.

Psalm 9:9-10 reminds us that the LORD is a refuge for the oppressed, the hurting, crushed, dejected, humbled, contrite, broken; a stronghold in times of trouble. Those who know His Name will trust Him, and He will never forsake those who seek Him. He is our hope. We are also reminded that God does not ignore the cries of the afflicted—the helpless.

In verse 18 David reminds us "the needy will not always be forgotten, nor the hope of the afflicted ever perish." Therefore, our hope is not found in our world system, our government, or other people. Although they may come to our aide in times of distress, our ultimate hope is found in God alone.

God's resources are never depleted. His patience never runs out. He never grows tired of your trial. He will not forsake you when the journey to recovery is long. He will neither forget you nor desert you. He is the reason for hope. He is hope. Trust God. Seek God. Believe God. Hang onto hope.

Hope for Daily Living

Have you ever lost enough in this life that you seemed to be able to do nothing except hang on? Losing possessions, friendships, family or health can cause you to lose the ability to function normally and often leave you emotionally paralyzed. When facing difficult situations, what will you do to hang onto hope?

Read Psalm 20:6-7. In times of crisis, have you trusted in anything other than God to meet your needs? In these verses, what does David say about trusting God?

Heavenly Father, You know there have been times in my life when circumstances could have destroyed me either emotionally or spiritually. But here I am, thanking you because of your mighty right hand that carried me through those difficult situations. LORD, help me remember that my security is not in houses and land, jobs or people, money or possessions. My security is in You alone. Grant me the strength and wisdom to seek You and trust You. And, Father, if a time comes when it seems my world is falling apart, infuse me with the courage to believe You and hang onto hope. I pray in the Name of Jesus. Amen.

Chapter four

Faith to Hope

But by faith
we eagerly await
through the
Spirit
the righteousness
for which we
hope.

Galatians 5:5

Even after decades of walking with Jesus, I stand amazed at God's perfect timing. As I look back through the years and recall days that were darker than a moonless sky, I am reminded of the powerful presence of God in each situation. At times, I did not recognize the Hand of God until long after my emotional healing began. At other times, I knew immediately that God's grace had powerfully prepared me to face my situation head on.

This morning I am once again profoundly aware of God's perfect timing. After another restless night pondering the news of a loved one's medical diagnosis, and as hopelessness tried to creep into my mind and my heart, I picked up the daily devotional book that I have read faithfully over the past ten years—*Streams in the Desert*.

Today's entry begins "There are times when everything looks very dark to me—so dark that I have to wait before I have hope. Waiting *with* hope is very difficult, but true patience is expressed when we must even wait *for* hope." – George Matheson

So, there it is. In faith, you and I must wait for hope. Until hope comes, you must have faith; belief, conviction, confidence in God and reliance and dependence on God. You must remember that just behind the dark clouds of fear is the sunshine of

God's love. You and I must believe the invisible in spite of the visible. We must practice what we often preach to others. Trust God!

Therefore, until hope comes, pray to our Heavenly Father for strength to stand firm in faith and wait for hope. Remind Him of what He already knows— You are weak. Cling to what you already know— He is strong!

I am aware of many facing a similar dilemma. You may be sitting beside your loved one in a hospital room or at home with the help of Hospice. Your income may have dried up but your creditors don't care. Your child may have lost his way, and you are not sure that it will be *only* temporary. You may be feeling the weight of hopelessness bending your shoulders toward the ground.

I have good news! You are not alone while you wait in faith for your hope to be restored.

So do not fear, for I am with you;
do not be dismayed, for I am your God.
I will strengthen you and help you;
I will uphold you with my righteous right hand.
Isaiah 41:10

In faith, hope on sweet friends!

Hope for Daily Living

Hebrews 11:1 says "faith is being sure of what we hope for and certain of what we do not see." Do you have that confidence in God? Explain

Read Hebrews 10:23. The original language for hold, or hold fast in some translations, means to keep in memory or retain the hope we profess. Do you believe God is faithful to fulfill His promises to His children? Do you remember a time when God intervened in your situation? Write it here.

Read Psalm 86:6-7. Do you, like David, believe God will hear and answer you when you call upon His Name? Why?

Are you willing to stand in faith and wait for hope?
Explain.

*Heavenly Father, life sometimes gets too hard to
bear. When that happens, it is easy to lose my
way—to forget you have promised to never leave me
or forsake me. Forgive me Lord when I fail to wait
in faith for hope. Remember, I am human and in the
darkness I forget. In the midst of the pain and
heartache, I grow anxious and afraid. In spite of all
I know about you, I sometimes step into the trap
satan has set for me. Lord, when I am dismayed,
strengthen me. When I fall, pick me up. When I am
afraid, give me courage. And when I am ashamed,
remind me there is no condemnation for those who
are in Christ Jesus. Only in You, and through You,
and by You do I have the faith to hope. Thank you
for loving me. I pray in the precious Name of Jesus.
Amen.*

Hope in God's Faithfulness

God has proven His faithfulness to me many, many times. This is one of my favorites.

I was required to update certification for my work in 2007, and my employer scheduled my classes in Las Vegas. The second morning there, I left the hotel in which I was staying to catch a bus to the other end of town for class. I got into a conversation with another lady and when the bus arrived, I got on with several other people including my supervisor. After the bus had traveled a short distance, I realized I did not have my purse with me. I immediately approached the driver and told him I needed off the bus.

Fast forward through our verbal exchange and my exit from the bus. As I started running down the street I began praying, telling God I trusted him to protect my purse. Then a small...quiet...calm voice asked, "If you trust me, why are you running?" I stopped running.

As I approached the bus stop, I saw my purse was not there. I <u>calmly</u> entered the hotel and went to the security desk. I <u>calmly</u> told the person behind the desk about leaving my purse and was beginning to give a description of it when I raised my head and saw my purse setting on a cabinet a few feet away.

I later learned that as I boarded the front of the bus, an employee of my hotel exited the rear. She saw my purse and dropped it off at the security desk. God's faithful intervention? I believe so!

—Ina
California

Chapter Five

Hope in Everything

Through Him

I can do everything

through Him

Who gives me

strength.

Philippians 4:13

Recently I was cleaning out our VHS, DVD, and CD collection. In the midst of the mess, I came across the DVD from my sweet sister's funeral; my heart sank. Moments later I picked up the DVD from my precious brother's funeral. I could feel myself sinking into a pit as satan stuck his knife in my heart and twisted.

Having been in that pit on previous occasions, I have learned to recognize the signs of a downward spiral and to immediately cry out the name of Jesus. When I reach for Him, He comes. He reminds me that I am His, and He is always near. When the fires of life are hot, He comes near with a refreshing breeze. When the waters of life are high, He carries me through the stormy waves.

When I walk through the dry desert, He is a cool drink of water. When the chaos of this world shatters my nerves, He speaks peace. And when I think I have nothing left to give, He reaches down, lifts me up, and reminds me that I am His, I am blessed, and I am able to do all things through Christ because He is my strength.

What brings satan with his sharpened blade twisting through your heart? What arid desert place are you walking through? Are you struggling to keep your head about the raging waves of a life storm that is rocking your world? There is hope in the midst of your crisis. His Name is Jesus. Call out to Him; for salvation, comfort, peace, wisdom, restoration… He will come, renew your strength, and revive your soul.

Hope for Daily Living

Has there been a time when you found yourself sinking deeper and deeper into a spiritual pit as a "life storm" raged around you? Explain.

Read Psalm 46:1. What does this verse tell you about living in fear in the midst of your storm?

Read Psalm 107:29. Do you believe God can/will still the storm in your life? Why or why not?

Read 2 Corinthians 5:9a. If God's answer during your storm is NO, will you trust Him to renew your strength and revive your soul?

Heavenly Father, although there are times when I feel overwhelmed by the storm in my life, your Word tells me that You are with me and able to carry me across every wave until You speak peace to the billowing tides that flood my soul. Lord, when I am fearful and anxious, remind me that I am safe with You, that You are in control, that You will rescue me, give me strength and protect me as you hide me under your wings. When life's storms swirl around me, I am never alone for You are my hiding place. Praising You in the Name of Jesus. Amen

Chapter Six

Hope

For Such A

Time as

This

And who knows

but that You

have come to royal

position for such a time as this?

Esther 4:14b

The closest I have ever come to royalty was during a trip to London where my husband and I walked the one-half mile red-surfaced road called The Mall. British flags, St. James Park, and the Queen's Guard stationed along the route leaves no doubt that Buckingham Palace lies ahead; standing in royal prominence. When the Queen is in residence, the Union Jack waves above the palace to announce Her Majesty's presence.

In front of the palace and just outside the gates, the Queen Victoria Memorial, standing eighty-two feet high and made of gleaming white marble, radiates as the sun smiles on its surface, and standing beneath her memorial while watching the Changing of the Guard drew me into a world that I could never have imagined.

The opulence of the gilded gates and proud stallions accompanied by the red and black clad soldiers and shining brass instruments of the marching band displayed a world I could only watch from the outside—never hoping to be invited in and certainly never thinking that I could be of any benefit to the people of the country of my ancestors. I am only a "commoner."

But God has a way of taking a common and ordinary person and turning her into an uncommon and extraordinary person. Such is the story of

Esther. A beautiful, young, Jewish virgin, orphaned and being raised by an uncle, snatched from her common life and thrust into the king's harem. Placed under the care of the king's eunuch, she was soaked in oils and spices, fed a special diet, and prepared for her night with the king. When it came, she won his favor and found herself positioned as Queen Esther.

Eventually, her uncle Mordecai made her aware of a plot to wipe out the Jews. He asked her to go before the King to save her people. Esther feared for her life for to go before the king without an invitation could mean immediate death. But Mordecai sent her a message, "Do not think that because you are in the king's house you alone of all the Jews will escape. For if you remain silent at this time, relief and deliverance for the Jews will arise from another place, but you and your father's family will perish. And who knows but that you have come to your royal position for such a time as this?" (Esther 4:13-14)

Esther responded to her uncle with a request for the Jewish people to fast and pray for three days. Then she would go before the king. On the third day, she dressed herself in royal garments and stood in the king's hall; waiting to be accepted or put to death. The king extended to her his gold scepter, and she entered his presence. By the end of the book of

Esther, we find that her request was granted, and the perpetrator of the annihilation plot along with his entire family were put to death; saving the Jews.

You may think this Biblical account of the life of a young Jewish orphan is not relevant to you. I would challenge that assumption. Today, just as in Esther's day, we fight similar battles. The circumstances may be different, but the battle remains the same; for it is "not against flesh and blood, but against the rulers, against the authorities, against the powers of this dark world and against the spiritual forces of evil in the heavenly realms? (Ephesians 6:12)

Often the battle appears overwhelming as more and more we see the cross of Christ and the Word of God trampled beneath the feet of our nation's legal system. It is possible family members may turn their backs as you answer the call of God on your life. Friends may drop like flies sprayed with bug killer as you find God walking through the pages of His Word.

But do not be deceived by the enemy. When you surrender your life to God through His Son Jesus Christ, you are royalty. You have access to the throne room and the power of the King of Kings. And King David reminded you and me in Psalm 139 that God has a plan for each life when he wrote,

"My frame was not hidden from you when I was made in the secret place, when I was woven together in the depths of the earth."

So never forget that although you may feel like a commoner; ordinary, average, typical—God can use you to do the uncommon; rare, unique, exceptional, extraordinary—when you surrender your life to be used for His glory. There is hope—"And, who knows but that you have come to royal position (*in Christ-mine*) for such a time as this?"

Hope for Daily Living

Have you ever been snatched out of familiar surroundings and thrust into uncertain circumstances? How did you respond?

Do you ever feel common, ordinary, average, or typical—believing God could never use you to impact someone's life? Read Ephesians 1:15-24. Write verses 19-21.

Do you desire to be uncommon—exceptional, extraordinary—for Christ? Read Ephesians 3:14-20. Write verse 20 here. Whose power will enable you to be uncommon and extraordinary for Christ

Read 2 Corinthians 2:14-15. Write what you read about the adequacy of God's grace for every situation.

Heavenly Father, Today, help me to remember that you are able—in every situation—to accomplish the task you have set before me. I can do everything you ask through Christ who gives me strength. When I feel common, remind me that I am Your child; royalty. My earthly heritage neither exempts me from nor elevates me to extraordinary living. It is my spiritual inheritance through Christ that enables me to say yes to a life of rare, unique, exceptional, extraordinary adventures with You. When I doubt, please remind me that You placed me in this time in history, and You are calling me to obedience for "such a time as this." Amen and Amen in the most precious Name of Jesus.

Chapter Seven

Hope in Times of

Depression

Why am I so depressed?

Why this turmoil within me?

Put your hope in God,

for I will still praise Him,

my Savior and my God.

Psalm 43:5 HCSB

During my morning talk with my Heavenly Father, I approached the matter of depression and anxiety. Recently, the word depressed and/or depression has flooded my conversations with family, friends, and acquaintances. Having been through a time of depression after the death of my baby sister, I have developed a deeper compassion for those who consistently struggle with anxiety and depression.

As I thought about reasons depression may be so prevalent in our society, I decided to check the morning headlines. Here is a short list of what I found:

MSN headlines June 2, 2016
UCLA gunman had accused slain professor of stealing his computer code, sources say
Remains of Missing 15-Year-Old Texas Girl Found Under Sink in Abandoned Apartment
PGA Tour golfer pulls out of tournament because of 'incredible anxiety'

San Antonio Express-News June 2, 2016
<u>Major highway shut down due to flooding near downtown S.A.</u>
Texas dad charged with DWI after child falls out of moving car
Man fatally shot near NW side apartments

Simply following the day's news is exhaustively depressing. Add to that your personal and family issues, and anxiety can drain your joy and happiness like an orange trapped in a juice squeezer.

I also found the "Anxiety and Depression Association of America." Their website listed several anxiety/depression disorders:

Generalized Anxiety Disorder (GAD)
Panic Disorder
Social Anxiety Disorder
Obsessive-Compulsive Disorder (OCD)
Posttraumatic Stress Disorder (PTSD)
Major Depressive Disorder
Persistent Depressive Disorder (PDD)
The website states that along with these disorders, co-occurrence of anxiety and other disorders may exist:

Bipolar disorder
Eating disorders
Headaches
Irritable bowel syndrome (IBS)
Sleep disorders
Substance abuse
Adult ADHD (attention deficit/hyperactive disorder)
BDD (body dysmorphic disorder)

Chronic pain
Fibromyalgia
Stress

My shoulders drooped as I read each list. I argued
with God about writing on this topic. After all, my
goal is to encourage, and I certainly find no
encouragement in this topic. I realize depression
and anxiety is a complicated emotional/medical
issue, and I am not qualified to address it on either
of those levels. But God began to remind me of the
hope that is found in Him.

So, if you are facing anxiety and/or depression, seek
professional help. There is no shame in finding a
godly doctor or counselor who can help you.
Christians are not immune from depression. Well-
meaning friends might tell you to "snap out of it."
But depression isn't something you can just "snap
out of."

Seek the Lord. There are many Scriptures that
address anxiety/depression, encourage, and give
hope. Remember, the best defense against anxiety is
a strong offense from God's Word. Here are a few
that may help:

Rejoice in hope; be patient in affliction; be
persistent in prayer. *Romans 12:12 (HCSB)*

Come to Me, all of you who are weary and burdened, and I will give you rest. *Matthew 11:28 (HCSB)*

Therefore, we may boldly say: The Lord is my helper; I will not be afraid. What can man do to me? *Hebrews 13:6 (HCSB)*

Also, Psalm 91, Psalm 92, and Psalm 139 will stir your heart to hope in The Almighty who created you, knows you, loves you, and is your help in time of trouble.

As I have already stated, I am not medically qualified to address issues of anxiety/depression. But, I know personally the God who created our bodies, and I hope you do as well. We have all sinned and come short of the glory of God. (Romans 3:23) The wages of that sin is death, but God's gift to us is eternal life in Christ. (Romans 6:23) Jesus is the Only Way to the Father. (John 14:6) God demonstrated His love for us when He sent His Only Son to die in our place. (Romans 5:8) And His Word tells us, "Whoever calls upon the name of the Lord shall be saved." (Romans 10:13) He is our hope in times of depression.

Hope for Daily Living

Read Psalm 121. Do you, or does someone you love, battle depression? Personalize this Psalm and write it here inserting your name or the name of your loved one.

Read Psalm 119:129-132. Do you believe God? Do you long to know and follow His commands? Pray these verses, and ask God to give you wisdom and understanding in the midst of any difficult situation you are facing. Write what He speaks to your heart.

Ephesians 1:3-10 assures us that God's redemption plan was set in motion before the creation of the world. Before Genesis 1:3 and God said…, before Adam and Eve…, before Moses on Mount Sinai… Immanuel, God With Us, was chosen (1 Peter 1:20.) Revelation 13:8 tells us the "Lamb that was slain from the creation of the world" is the One to whom the Book of Life belongs.

Do you trust Him? Do you believe Him? Will your seek Him? Will you be a follower of Christ, even when the answer to your prayers is NO? Do you love Him?

Why am I so depressed?
Why this turmoil within me?
Put your hope in God, for I will
Still praise Him,
My Savior and my God
Psalm 43:5 HCSB

Heavenly Father, I believe Your arm is long, Your hand is mighty, and You are filled with compassion for those who trust You. Today, I allow You to be my Strong Tower; the place to which I run during times of anxiety or depression. I put my hope in You. I praise you. I trust You for wisdom, direction, and strength in my time of need. I pray in the precious Name of Jesus and for Your glory. Amen and Amen.

Hope When Depression Hurts

My heart is troubled. Sometimes I wish I didn't have such giant feelings. I know it makes me who I am, and God made me that way, but I still don't like it; at times feeling like I let someone down, and that's a horrible feeling.

You have no idea how much the prayers of friends help. And if you are struggling too, know I'm lifting you up. As many of you know, it's a battle. And sometimes I think as a Christian it's harder because we know God's promises to never leave us or forsake us are so true. It's not that we don't want to be happy or feel joy. It's a physical thing that overtakes your mind.

I hate depression! It robs you of so much. I try hard not to let it, but some days are just harder than others. I hope by sharing my struggle today it has helped someone in some way. Please whisper a prayer for me and anyone else you know who suffers from depression.

—Angie
Tennessee

Chapter Eight

Hope in Knowing
Jesus is...

In the beginning was the Word,

and the Word was with God,

and the Word was God.

He was with God in the beginning.

Through him all things were made;

without him nothing was made

that has been made.

In Him was life, and that life

was the light of men.

The light shines in the darkness,

but the darkness has not understood it.

John 1:1-5

Who is Jesus…

He is:

> The Son of God
> The Word of God
> God—made visible to man
> Creator
> Life
> Light

Jesus is not a created being but rather "In the beginning" already with God.

He is:

The Almighty—nothing is impossible for Him (Revelation 1:8)

The Author and Finisher of our faith—fix your eyes on Him (Hebrews 12:2)

The Bread of Life—depend on Him for daily sustenance (John 6:32-35)

The Bright Morning Star—in His light, we cannot lose our way (Revelation 22:16)

The Door—He is the only way to heaven (John 10:9)

Emmanuel—God with us (Matthew 1:23)

Our Hope—He is our only source of hope in this world (1 Timothy 1:1)

He is the Lamb of God, the King of Kings, the Light of the World, the Lord of Lords, Messiah. His Name is Jesus, the Greek form of Yeshua (Joshua) and His Name means Jehovah is salvation. HE IS OUR HOPE!

Hope: living in expectation of what God is going to bring about in my life and the lives of those for whom I pray, through His Son Jesus Christ, Messiah, Lord.

If you belong to God through salvation found in Christ alone, you are forgiven, rescued, redeemed, chosen, accepted, saved, loved, alive and free. Hope should be a natural outcome of knowing who Jesus is and who you are in Him.

If your heart is broken today, if you are consumed by depression, if you are filled with unforgiveness or anger, if… (fill in your heartache) whisper Jesus. He is alive, and He loves you!

Hope for Daily Living

Because of Jesus, I am eternally secure. Read Romans 8:1-17 How does knowing you have eternal security through Jesus Christ, change the way you view life's heartaches and struggles? Or does it?

Write your personal testimony of your salvation experience. If you cannot, please see the salvation Scriptures in the back of this book.

Heavenly Father, today I am grateful for the gift of Your Son Jesus, through whom I have eternal security. My hope is found in Christ alone. Through Him I am sealed, secure, and victorious. I cannot be beaten or stopped. Even in death, I win! Praise His Name. Amen and Amen

Chapter Nine

Hope for the

Captive Heart

The Spirit of the Lord is upon me,

because he hath anointed me

to preach the gospel

to the poor;

he hath sent me to

heal the brokenhearted,

to preach

deliverance to the captives,

and recovering of sight to the blind,

to set at liberty

them that are bruised,

Luke 4:18 KJV

The guard lowered a bucket on a rope from his perch in the tower outside the fifteen-foot razor-wire-topped chain-link fence. Each of us dropped our driver's license into the bucket and watched as the guard pulled it upward. Satisfied with our identities, he returned each license following the same process.

We then stepped through a gate into a wire cage between two rows of razor-wire-topped fencing. As that gate locked behind us, the entrance to the prison yard opened. Once inside the prison, each of us signed the registration sheet with name, purpose, and driver's license number.

The chaplain escorted us down the hall and into the cage where an officer took our driver's licenses for photo identification purposes. The huge iron bars clanged closed behind us. Only then did the iron gate that opened onto the hallway leading to the chapel release us to walk our sound equipment into our place of ministry.

For a brief moment in time, we were captive.

As I turned and looked down the hall behind us, I caught a glimpse of a sign attached to a wall of iron; "You are now entering Death Row." Over four hundred men lived behind that iron wall. My heart sank as I thought about their fate then jumped for joy with hopeful expectation of what God might do in the hearts of the broken, bruised, captives who would hear His Word presented on that night.

I soon discovered God's presence saturating the chapel as many men in white raised their hands and unashamedly praised the Lord. Their bodies held captive. Their hearts set free. I thought about men and women outside prison walls who walk freely in society but are often held captive by sin, heartache, sorrow, and pain.

The Greek word translated bruise in this verse is thrauō; to be oppressed, downtrodden or broken in pieces. Is that you? Are you oppressed, downtrodden, burdened, abused…? Is your life broken? Are you held captive by sin, grief, illness? Have you built an iron cage around your heart?

Hopefully, you will never know the sadness of prison incarceration. Yet, how much greater the sadness of a heart held captive. I have great news! There is hope for your captive heart. His name is Jesus, and He has come to set you free. He can put the broken pieces of your life together and heal your captive heart. Believe Him. Accept Him. Trust Him.

Hope for Daily Living

There is an old saying that goes: "The gem cannot be polished without friction, nor the man (woman) perfected without trials. Have the trials in your life held your heart captive or perfected you in your walk with God? Explain.

"You are my refuge and my shield; I have put my hope in your word." Psalm 119:114. When doubt or fear assault your emotions, do you run to God's Word for refuge, or do you allow those emotions to take your heart and mind captive?

Read Acts 2:26. What does it mean to "rest in hope?"

Heavenly Father, today help me to realize there is rest in hope because my hope is in Christ alone. I have peace with you, Father, because of my faith in Jesus. Help me to persevere in hope to your glory. Hope in you will keep my heart free from the captivity of this world. Help me to be joyful in hope, patient in affliction, and faithful in prayer. In Jesus Name. Amen and Amen

Chapter Ten

Hope When You Do It

God's Way

The Word of the LORD
came to Jonah...Go
To the great city of Nineveh
and preach against it...
But Jonah ran away
from the LORD
and headed for Tarshish.

Jonah 1:1-3

When I was eight years old, my mother and I bounced around in the top last row of a Greyhound double-decker bus from Michigan to Tennessee. Sliding left and right and jolting up and down for several hundred miles left a lasting impression on my stomach.

However, by day two at my grandparent's house, my stomach returned to normal, and I was stepping on grandpa's heels as he went about the business of working the farm. I kept noticing him tearing a piece of a dark substance off a block of something he pocketed in his bib overalls. He would put it in his mouth, chew, spit, and wipe his lips with the back of his hand. It looked good, so I kept asking, "Can I have some?" He continued to reply, "No," until he became weary of my asking.

Finally, he tore off a small piece and handed it to me with careful instructions to not swallow either the juice or the plug of tobacco. I promised! Unfortunately, without thinking, I swallowed. I turned green. I gagged. I vomited. Grandpa smiled. He knew I would never again ask for a "chaw" of his tobacco. Lesson learned!

Jonah also learned a lesson. God called him to preach to the city of Nineveh "because its wickedness has come up before me." (Jonah 1:2) Apparently, Jonah did not like what the LORD had to say and chose to run rather than obey. He went to the port of Joppa, paid his fare, and boarded a ship bound for Tarshish; according to maps of the then-known world, that was as far as he could go in the opposite direction.

God sent a storm, the crew threw Jonah overboard, a great fish swallowed Jonah, the seas calmed, and after three days in the belly of that great fish and a powerful prayer, Jonah was vomited onto dry ground. Again, the word of the LORD came to Jonah "Go to the great city of Nineveh and proclaim to it the message I give you." This time Jonah obeyed! The city repented, God showed compassion, and destruction was averted.

Sometimes we get what we ask for only to find out it is not good for us. Sometimes we run from God. Sometimes our disobedience impacts others. And like my grandfather's "yes" to my request for tobacco, God sometimes allows us to learn the hard way. But God is the God of second chances. There is always hope when you run *to* Him rather than *from* Him. What is He asking of you?

Hope for Daily Living

Have you ever run from God? If yes, what was the result?

Read Psalm 25:21 and write it here.

Read Psalm 69:6. Do you believe your actions and/or attitudes can cause others to lose hope? Explain.

Heavenly Father, I understand that my life belongs to you alone. I realize that my actions and attitudes might alter others' conception of You, Mighty God. Help me as I strive to follow Christ and in doing so, correctly display your grace to all. I ask You in the most precious Name of Jesus. Amen and Amen.

God's Peace Gives Hope in an Unexpected Storm

Can we experience God's peace when an unexpected storm arises? Absolutely

May 29th of 2000 started out as any other day at youth camp near Livingston, Texas, and I was participating in the games, worship, and meals and having a great time celebrating my son Chris's sixteenth birthday with his fellow students. David and I and our children attended Metropolitan Baptist Church in Houston, and I always went to youth camp as a counselor. That summer, my daughter Lisa had just finished her sophomore year in college, and she was on a mission trip with her college ensemble in Germany. David was home in

Houston working, and this was just a normal summer week for us.

During the evening worship service, one of the camp employees approached me and said that I had an emergency phone call in the office. When I got to the office, my husband was on the phone telling me that my mom was having emergency surgery the following morning in Baytown, Texas.

She had fallen while visiting friends in the Methodist Hospital downtown, and when they did an MRI to determine how much repair work was needed for a broken hip, they discovered that she had multiple myeloma, and the cancer had eaten through the bone in her hip. She was going to be having total hip replacement, and begin the process of meeting with the cancer doctors, etc.

My brother and dad were requesting me to come immediately to help with care for my mom and decisions that needed to be made. My dad was handicapped and used a walker to get around because of multiple back injuries and nerve damage, so I knew he wanted me to be able to be places where he would not be able to get around. I immediately began to pray, "God, I know you knew this was coming, and I know you have a plan." I approached our youth minister and told him that I needed to leave camp that night if possible.

It just so happened (God was already providing) that Buddy Riddle, a retired Houston police officer who had surrendered to ministry was at camp. He offered to drive me half-way home to meet my husband. As we discussed how the events had transpired, he said, "I kept asking God all week. Why do

you have me at this camp this week?
There is so much I need to be doing
back at the church office in Houston?
Now I know; He wanted me here to
take you to your husband in the
middle of the night." We discussed how
God is always there ahead of us and
knows what we need. **Phil: 4:4-7** says,
"Don't worry about anything. Instead,
pray about everything. Tell God your
needs and don't forget to thank Him
for His answers. If you do this, you
will experience God s peace which
surpasses human understanding."
(Living Bible translation)

I began to pray **James 1:5-7** "If any of
you lacks wisdom, you should ask God,
who gives generously to all without
finding fault, and it will be given to
you. But let him ask in faith
without doubting for the one
who doubts is like the surf of the sea
driven and tossed by the wind. For let

not that man expect that he will receive anything from the Lord, being a double-minded man, unstable in all his ways." I had no idea what the days ahead would hold for me, I just knew God was in control.

I arrived home around midnight, and got up early the next morning to drive to Baytown. We arrived 10 minutes before Mom went in to surgery, and I was able to see her. She hugged my neck and said, "You know God has this under control, don't you?" I immediately felt a peace that I knew only God could give, and said, "Yes, Mom, I know." She reminded me of Scripture that she had often quoted when I was growing up, "What time I am afraid, I will trust in Thee." Psalms 56: 3, KJV.

My mom came through surgery fine, and we met with the cancer doctor the next morning. It was determined that Mom would start receiving radiation treatments while recovering from hip surgery because the doctors wanted to shrink the cancer as much as they could before beginning chemotherapy. They let us know that Mom would be in the hospital at least four to six weeks. I turned to David and said, "I think I'm going to need to stay here to be with Mom. Can you manage the kids and everything?"

He's always been my prince, and he answered, "We will get things taken care of here." Our daughter was flying in from Germany that evening, but her flight was coming into Dallas instead of Houston because there had been a complication with the airplane. So, my husband's brother Donnie and his wife Terry offered to drive to Dallas to pick up Lisa and bring her to Baytown. Once again, God was showing me how he was providing for my needs in the midst of the storm.

My devotion the next morning was on Proverbs 16:3, "Commit to the Lord whatever you do, and he will establish your plans." As I began to pray about what God wanted me to do for Mom and Dad, I decided I needed to check in with the school where I taught and let them know what was happening. I called my friend Pam Edwards, Director of Instruction at Windfern High School in Cypress Fairbanks, and explained the situation and said that I was probably going to have to quit my job to be able to care for my mom. We talked for a couple of hours, and she said that she would let our principal Marvin Webster know the details the next morning. They were both Christians, and I knew they were praying for me.

The next morning, when I came back
to Mom's room after going to radiation
treatment with her, my principal
Marvin Webster was sitting in the
sitting room attached to Mom's
hospital room. He said, "You are not
going to quit. I've already talked to
personnel, and made arrangements for
you to speak with the family medical
leave administrator, and you will be
able to come here when your mom is in
the hospital, and you can work when
you don't need to be here. God was
confirming to me that he was in
control, and I was reminded of
Proverbs 16:9, "In their hearts humans
plan their course, but the Lord
establishes their steps." NIV.
Mom stayed in the hospital for six
weeks that summer doing rehab on her
hip and receiving radiation
treatments. Then, once at home, she
began receiving chemo treatments
once a month for three months at a

time. She would stay in the hospital for three days for each treatment; then, she would be at home for the next month. Dad was able to make her meals during the day, and her Bible study class of young adults that she had taught for about five years before her illness, provided meals for her and dad at least three days a week. I was able to stay with her the six weeks while she was in the hospital and for three weeks once she went home.

Then, once she and dad felt comfortable, I was able to come home and start school. I was able to take off every time she had chemo and stay with her in the hospital. These were precious times that we were able to spend together and we talked during all hours of the night when she could not sleep. In addition, because my son had turned sixteen on the day that mom was diagnosed, he immediately

was able to drive himself to summer
band and anywhere else he needed to
be. My daughter worked with my
husband that summer, so the three of
them would come visit me after work
about once a week. The hospital was
about an hour and a half from our
home in Houston.

Mom went into remission after one
year of radiation and chemo
treatments, and we tried to make
memories with her for the entire
family. After a year of remission, the
cancer returned, and she started
treatments again. Once again, I was
able to be with her for the treatments
and any care that she needed because
of the generosity of my boss. She lived
for four years after being diagnosed
with the cancer. She would witness to
all of the hospital personnel she
encountered, and she would ask them
how she could pray for them. She was

able to pray for a physical therapist whose fiancé had the same cancer that Mom had.

During Mom's entire illness, our family tried to focus on how God was working in the situation and not the situation itself. Instead of praying for healing, Mom asked us to pray that we would be witnesses for Him and that God would be glorified in the situation. She said if He chose to heal her, that would be great, but she was more concerned about us seeing Him work in our lives and in every little detail of this ordeal. We started keeping a journal of instances where we knew God had intervened on our behalf. We were able to experience joy and peace as we watched for ways God was moving in the circumstances.

We all became stronger in our faith and dependence on God because we

could see Him working every
day. **Romans 8:26-27** says, "In the same
way, the Spirit helps us in our
weakness. We do not know what we
ought to pray for, but the Spirit
himself intercedes for us through
wordless groans. And he who searches
out hearts knows the mind of the
Spirit, because the Spirit intercedes for
God's people in accordance with the
will of God." NIV.

When people ask me if I'm sorry I had
to go through this experience, I always
say, "No, because I learned so much
about how God knows our needs before
we ask, and His provisions are
sufficient, and the peace He gives
surpasses our understanding. He just
wants us to ask. Matthew 7:7 says,
"Ask and it will be given to you; seek
and you will find; knock and the door
will be opened to you." NIV.

Two years after Mom passed away, when we cleaned out hers and Dad's house for Dad to move, we found a note in the prayer bucket on the table that had been written by Mom on September 13, 2000. It said, "I give myself-emotional, spiritual, and physical being to God to do as He chooses. To heal, or not heal, to suffer more cancer cells or less, whatever He chooses for my lot in life for the remaining years, months, or days left to me at 71 + years."

God confirmed to me, once again, we are His children, and He will meet us in the storms of life. We just need to remember to seek His face and pray that our lives go in His ways, not our own.

—Melanie
Texas

Chapter Eleven

Hope When I

Want to

Give up!

"I am the LORD,
the God of all mankind.
Is anything
too hard for me?"

Jeremiah 32:27

Today, the Lord planted the words "Don't Give Up" in my heart. I found a Scripture appropriate to the title and waited for inspiration. Nothing! I tried to write about areas in life where giving up may seem the best option. Nothing! I prayed and asked God to inspire me. Nothing!

I went to the laundry room to take clothes out of the dryer and throw them on the dining room table; my mind in deep contemplation as my body went through the necessary motions. I began to think about changing topics, but once again God spoke softly in my spirit, "Don't Give Up."

Finally, I got it! God was inspiring me by pushing me to the brink of giving up in order to get the message. "Don't Give Up." I wondered how many lost opportunities in life happened because I gave up right before success. How often did I see a situation as hopeless when God had a breakthrough waiting right around the corner? How many times did I assume the answer was no while God's yes waited for my faithful perseverance?

I began to think about the characteristics of God, trying to remember if He had ever given up on me. He has not! He reminded me-

He is Able…..
He is Faithful…..
He is Merciful…..
He is God Who Sees…..
He is God Who Forgives…..
He is God My Exceeding Joy…..
He is God My Righteousness…..
He is The Lord My Redeemer…..
He is The Lord My Defense…..
He is The Lord Mighty in Battle…..

And He is the God Who NEVER GIVES UP! So, when like me you are tempted to throw in the towel, hang it up, or weasel out, remember the One who gave all for you, and Don't Give Up!

Hope for Daily Living

Do you wish you could give up on something or someone? Explain.

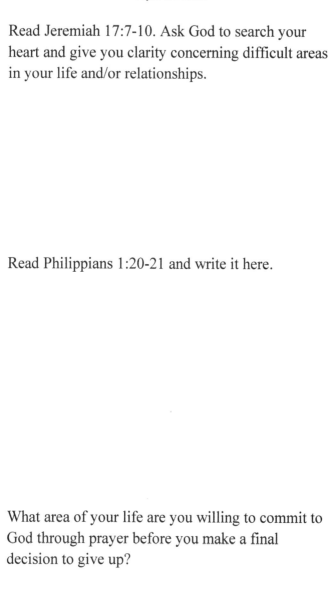

Read Jeremiah 17:7-10. Ask God to search your heart and give you clarity concerning difficult areas in your life and/or relationships.

Read Philippians 1:20-21 and write it here.

What area of your life are you willing to commit to God through prayer before you make a final decision to give up?

Commit to pray about it. Write your prayer here.

Heavenly Father, I know that You are able, faithful, and merciful. I know that You see me, and You are my defense in battle. Today, I trust You with the difficult circumstances of my life. I believe You are my Righteous Redeemer and my Exceeding Great Joy. Help me, Lord, to hear and obey Your voice. In the precious Name of Jesus. Amen and Amen.

Chapter Twelve

Hope

For the

Battle

Put on the full armor

of God

so that you can take your stand

against the

devil's schemes.

Ephesians 6:11

Roman soldiers, when marching into battle, carried a shield approximately four and one-half feet long by two and one-half feet wide. Usually made of three sheets of wood glued together and covered with canvas and leather, the shield protected the soldier from his chin to his knees. During times of siege, the soldiers would gather in a "tortoise" formation shaping a rectangle with shields raised around the perimeter.

The soldiers in the center would lift their shields, resting them on the Roman helmets and overlapping in order to prevent arrows from penetrating their tortoise-like shell. In this manner, the entire formation stood strong and protected from the enemy.

When writing to the church at Ephesus, the Apostle Paul explained how, in the Christian life, we battle against spiritual forces. He used the wardrobe of the Roman soldier, something with which the people of Ephesus would have been familiar, to explain how to use the armor of God.

Paul not only listed the shield, but told the church to "put on the full armor of God…" then proceeded to list the necessary items:

The belt of truth
The breastplate of righteousness
Feet fitted with the gospel of peace
The shield of faith
The helmet of salvation
The sword of the Spirit, which is the Word of God

And in verse eighteen he added:

"And pray in the Spirit on all occasions with all kinds of prayers and requests. With this in mind, be alert and always keep on praying for all the saints."

Here, Paul outlined what I like to call the Spiritual Tortoise Shell. After putting on all the armor, pray—in the Spirit—on all occasions—with all kinds of prayers and requests. And, do not forget to be alert, watchful, and attentive. Watch out for the snares or attacks of the enemy. And *always* keep on praying for *all* the saints."

While this letter was written to the church at Ephesus, it was also intended for circulation among other churches. In this manner, the Apostle Paul emphasized the need for both individual submission to Christ as well as love, mercy, charity, and kindness toward all the saints—fellow believers and followers of Christ—through constant prayer.

Although written nearly two thousand years ago, these instructions remain valid and necessary. What would happen in our world today if every person who has surrendered to Christ as Lord would follow the instructions to keep on praying, in the Spirit, for all the saints? I hope the next time the enemy sets his sights on me, my fellow Christians will have me covered with a spiritual tortoise shell because of their constant prayers. God's armor is our hope for the battle.

Hope for Daily Living

Which piece of God's armor do you daily depend on? Explain.

Which piece of armor might you need to polish a bit? How do you know?

Read Ephesians 6:13. Write it here.

Today's political climate is becoming increasingly antagonistic towards Christians. Are you willing to stand, if necessary, against the assault of the enemy? Explain.

Heavenly Father, I know that You have spoken to me through the words of the Apostle Paul who at first fearlessly fought against You but later intimately and faithfully served you—even unto death. Lord, teach me to pray for my fellow brothers and sisters in Christ. Remind me that you do not see the color of our skin or the landscape of our residence but rather you see lives covered by the blood of Jesus; hearts forgiven of sin, and a life in right standing with You. Thank You for the Sword of the Spirit which is the Word of God. Help me to pray always for the saints and to be a part of Your "Spiritual Tortoise Shell" of protection. In the most precious Name of Jesus, Amen.

Chapter Thirteen

Called

To Hope

I pray also that the eyes

of your heart

may be enlightened

in order that you may

know the hope

to which

He has called you.

Ephesians 1:18a

Decades ago I had a hemorrhage in the retina of my left eye. Unfortunately, by the time I saw the doctor and he diagnosed the problem, it was too late to remedy the situation. He tried blood thinners which only exacerbated my problem and sent me for a short stay in the hospital.

Over the years, I have hoped that new technology would allow me to have improved vision in that eye. However, I have been told no technology exists to correct my problem. So I continue to see gray splotches through my left eye. My body has compensated for the inadequacies and while going through my daily routine, I rarely notice the issue; reading and depth perception create the most difficult challenges.

Recently, while reading Ephesians 1:18, the words "eyes of your heart may be enlightened" seemed to jump off the page. I thought about my physical vision and how wonderful it would be to have the injured eye enlightened; no more gray spots. Illuminated.

In his letter to the church at Ephesus, the Apostle Paul painted a beautiful picture of what happens when you allow Christ to become Lord of your life. His Holy Spirit moves into your heart shining His light that the "eyes of your heart" may be enlightened, informed, made aware, educated, and become grounded in the spiritual things of God. He does this so you may *know*—possess information, recognize, realize and understand— the *hope* to which He has called you.

Once you and I believe Christ for salvation, we are not left to flounder like a fish out of water. Our hope lies in who we are in Christ. God's Holy Spirit illuminates our heart in order that we may know the hope to which we are called.

We are justified – declared not guilty of sin
We are sanctified – made holy and acceptable in Jesus Christ
We are righteous – in right standing with God through Christ
We are blessed – with every spiritual blessing
We are forgiven – our sin taken away

We can now come boldly before God's throne of grace. (Hebrews 4:16) While we walk this earth, we are in God's care. When we leave this earth, we will see God face-to-face! He has called you, and he has called me, to know the *hope* that is found in Christ alone!

So today, let His power work its mighty strength in you so that "the eyes of your heart may be enlightened in order that you may know the hope to which He has called you."

Hope for Daily Living

Do you have the assurance of the hope to which God has called you? Explain.

List the spiritual blessings found in the following Scriptures:

Romans 8:1

1 Corinthians 1:2

Galatians 3:28

Ephesians 1:3

Ephesians 1:5,6

Ephesians 1:13

Colossians 2:10

Write Ephesians 1:18 here:

Heavenly Father, Thank you for calling me to hope in you through Jesus Christ Your Son. Thank you for including me in your family and for blessing me with all the spiritual blessings found in Christ. Thank you for placing your Holy Spirit inside of me to illuminate and enlighten my heart and mind in order that I may see your world through spiritual eyes and understand with a spiritual mind. Thank you that you will never let me go. I praise you in the precious Name of Jesus. Amen!

(If you cannot pray this prayer, I urge you to bow before a Holy God and ask Jesus Christ into your heart—right now. Scriptures to help may be found on page 223. I am praying for you.)

Chapter Fourteen

Equipped

For

Hope

All Scripture is
God-breathed
and is useful
for teaching, rebuking, correcting
and training in righteousness,
so that the man of God
may be thoroughly equipped
for every good work.

2 Timothy 3:16-17

Every day we witness circumstances of people equipped for action. Whether it be big-league sports, the medical profession, those who work in finance, construction, customer service or a myriad of other jobs, leaders and workers are most successful when they are well-equipped, furnished with the tools they need, armed with information, and appointed to the correct position to carry out the task at hand.

2 Timothy 3:16-17 tells us that "all Scripture is God-breathed and is useful for teaching, rebuking, correcting and training in righteousness." Because God has given us the tools we need to be thoroughly furnished for every circumstance in life, we are equipped to hope.

Romans 5:18 records that "Against all hope, Abraham *in hope believed* and so became the father of many nations…" Joshua 6:23 tells us that Rahab had hope in the promise of two spies from Israel— "the young men who had done the spying went in and brought out Rahab, her father and mother and brothers and all who belonged to her…" Because she hoped, waited in expectation, her family was saved from annihilation as the walls of Jericho collapsed around them.

1 Samuel 1 tells the story of Hannah. She longed for a child. She grieved and fasted while calling upon the LORD to answer her prayer for a child. Verse nineteen tells us "Elkanah lay with Hannah his wife, and the LORD remembered her." Verse twenty describes what happened next, "So in the course of time Hannah conceived and gave birth to a son. She named him Samuel, saying, 'Because I asked the LORD for him.'"

Throughout God's Word, we read the truth of life after life changed by believing God. What does that mean for you and me? How are we equipped for hope? We find the answer to those questions within the Word of God:

Believe on the Lord Jesus Christ and you will be saved. (Acts 16:31)
Trust in the LORD not yourself. Acknowledge Him in everything you do. (Proverbs 3:5-6)
Study to know the truth. (2 Timothy 2:15)
Glory in the cross alone. (Galatians 6:14)
Pray without ceasing. (1 Thessalonians 5:17)

Simply put, developing this pattern of living means believing God. I cannot begin to explain the number of ways I fail. I praise God that He does not seek human perfection but rather sees you and me in right standing with Him once we kneel at the cross and come to Him through the blood of His One and Only Begotten Son—Jesus. It is then, and only then, that we are equipped to hope!

Hope for Daily Living

Do you believe <u>in God</u> or do you <u>believe God</u>? Write James 2:19. Explain.

Write James 2:23. What is the difference between believing in God and believing God?

Read 1 Thessalonians 5:17. What does it mean to pray without ceasing?

Heavenly Father, Thank you that as Your child I can be equipped for hope and can wait in expectation as You work out Your best for me. Forgive me when I grow impatient. Show mercy when I struggle in the waiting. Teach me to believe You, trust You, and glory in the cross alone. In the precious Name of Jesus and for His glory. Amen and Amen.

Chapter Fifteen

Strength

to

Hope

When a strong man,

Fully armed,

guards his own house,

His possessions

are safe.

Luke 11:21

We live in a tumultuous time in world history. Daily we see the overt actions of aggression and hatred from an enemy who desires our complete annihilation. FBI 2012 Crime Clock Statistics finds that in 2012, a violent crime occurred every 26.0 seconds. A property crime occurred every 3.5 seconds. Many of these crimes occurred when innocent victims were at home, watching TV, eating dinner, doing laundry, washing dishes; feeling safe.

Hopelessness is evident as seen in the American Foundation for Suicide Prevention statistics stating "suicide is the 10th leading cause of death in the US; each year 42,773 Americans die by suicide."

Our world appears to be knee deep in the quick sand of anxiety, depression, and hopelessness. So, how do you, and how do I overcome being consumed by the fear and anxiety of the "what if?"

Luke 11:21 can be seen as instructions for safeguarding your heart against the enemy:

1. Be Strong
2. Be Fully Armed
3. Be On guard

Be Strong—Ephesians 6:10 explains that we can be strong in the Lord "and in his mighty power." We fight our battle on our knees. The battle is not against flesh and blood, but against the enemy of your soul. Your strength does not come from within but from the Almighty. He will give you the strength you need for the battle at hand.

When I read that verse I am reminded of a friend whose young son came running into the house shouting that the car had fallen on his daddy. My friend rushed outside to find her husband squashed between the driveway and the vehicle. Without thinking, she grabbed hold of the bumper, lifted the car, and held on until her two young sons pulled their father free. A couple of days later she grabbed that same bumper and tried to lift the car. It would not budge! God had given her the strength for the battle at hand. He will do the same for you.

Be Fully Armed—Ephesians 6:13-17 is a reminder to put on the "full armor of God." The belt of truth. The breastplate of righteousness. Feet fitted with the gospel of peace. The shield of faith. The helmet of salvation. The sword of the Spirit; the Word of God. Battles are rarely expected. The enemy usually sneaks up on you. Fired. Cancer. Anger. Bankruptcy. Fear. Death. Illness. Infidelity. Depression. Infertility. Be proactive—prepared, ready, trained. Every morning, put on the full armor of God.

Be On Guard—finally, when you are standing strong in God's power, and you are proactively dressed for battle, you should guard your own house. Because you are dressed in the armor of God and standing in the strength of God, you have the ability to overcome the enemy—satan. We guard our house as we "pray in the Spirit on all occasions." (Ephesians 6:18)

Never forget—when you are a child of the Living God, you do not fight your battles alone. Isaiah 26:3 reminds us, "Thou wilt keep him in perfect peace, whose mind is *stayed* (to be braced, steadfast, rely upon, gain confidence) on thee: because he trusteth in thee." KJV

Our hope against the attack of the enemy is to be strong, be fully armed, and be on guard; keep your mind confidently focused on the Father. There is hope in the midst of the battle, knowing we are safe, when we allow God, in His mighty power, to fight for us. He is our strength to hope!

Hope for Daily Living

Do you currently have a fear or anxiety? Explain.

If that fear, or the circumstance causing you
anxiety, became reality, what would you do?

Read Matthew 28:20, Psalm 34:18, and 1 Peter 5:7.
Write the verse that ministers to your current
circumstance or the circumstance of someone for
whom you are praying.

Are you willing to commit to time with the Father
every day, reading/studying His Word to you? (*You
may already do this. If so, are you willing to add ten
minutes to that amount of time?*) Write your
commitment here.

Precious Heavenly Father, in the Name of Jesus, I come to You today praising You because You alone are Almighty God. You are worthy of my praise, and I glorify You as the One and Only True God. I thank You that because You are my God, no enemy can triumph over me as I put my trust in You. Father, help me to safeguard my heart by believing You, trusting You, and standing firm on Your Word. Teach me to be strong, fully armed, and on guard against the enemy at all times. Remind me daily that through You, even when life appears hopeless, I have the strength to hope in the Name of Jesus. Amen.

Heartache, Healing, Hope

On January 16, 2001 at 6:30 a.m. while on my way to work at an orthodontist office in Dallas, Texas, my car was T-boned by a sixteen- passenger van running a red light. Police officer, Sgt. Sam, heard the impact from down the road at Starbucks.

I am told that as they were cutting the roof off my car, I told them I was a single mom and that they needed to get my nine-year-old son, Jacob to my brother and sister-in-law's house. I gave them all the address and phone number information, but I do not remember doing that.

At Parkland Hospital, they found my aorta ripped, among other injuries. I had seven surgeries in two and one-half months, ten pins in my left hip, and three in my left knee. The right side of my face is metal. My eye socket was crushed by the airbag.

My parents came from Tennessee for six months to take care of Jacob and me. I had years of physical therapy. The doctors said I would not walk again, but I did not believe them. I never felt like I would die. One really finds out what your true foundation is made of when something like that happens.

My normal no longer consisted of working fifty hours a week or being leader of the girls club (Awanas) at church, or secretary for the Wylie Sports Association, or helping my son to get his homework done, or taking him to football practice. Life as I knew it came to a screeching halt.

In the aftermath of the accident I felt Jesus wrap me up in His arms like a mother holds a newborn. I focused on my faith. That was all I had. I was on a honeymoon with my Savior.

For years I was doing very well, but

the last two years have brought arthritis and pain. While heartache brought me closer to God, healing has allowed distractions back in my life, and I miss the closeness I had with God during that time.

I know God would want me to share my testimony, and I feel blessed to have it to share. I hope you are encouraged after reading what God has done in my life.

—Patricia
Texas

Chapter Sixteen

Hope

In an

Alabaster

Jar

Jesus said

to the woman,

"Your faith has saved you;

go in peace."

Luke 7:50

In chapter seven of Luke's gospel, we see the interaction between Jesus and a never-named sinful (likely a prostitute) woman. Invited to dinner by a Pharisee, Jesus reclined at a low dining table, as was the custom. The shock of seeing a woman of such low reputation come to a Pharisee's house must have reverberated throughout the room.

Although a common custom to allow such dinners to be attended by spectators, it is unlikely that anyone would have expected a prostitute to attend. Yet there she stood; an Alabaster jar of precious perfume in hand. Weeping. Wailing. Mourning. (Translated from the Greek word klaiō.) Historians tell us the likely value of the precious perfume—a year's wages.

As she wept, her tears covered the feet of Jesus. That's when it happened! With the entire group of important men watching in horror, she loosened her hair, wiped then kissed the feet of Jesus, broke the neck of the alabaster jar, and poured the contents on Jesus' feet.

When the Pharisee who had invited Jesus to the dinner saw this, *he began talking to himself*, "If this man were a prophet, he would know who is touching him and what kind of woman she is—that she is a sinner." No doubt whispering under his breath, he must have been shocked when... Verse 40—*Jesus answered him*, "Simon, I have something to tell you."

Jesus then pointed out Simon's lack of concern when Jesus arrived at the dinner and was given none of the customary greetings. Not a kiss. No water to wash dusty feet. No common anointing oil for His head. And then the words that started the whole room talking; verse 48: Jesus said to *her*, "your sins are forgiven."

And while the astonished guests questioned "Who is this that even forgives sins," Jesus said to that never-named woman, "Your faith has saved you; go in peace."

So what can you, and what can I learn from this never-named woman who held onto hope in an alabaster jar? I'm sure she must have hoped that she could even get in the door at the dinner. She must have hoped for an opportunity to see Jesus. Perhaps she hoped against all hope that she would actually get near enough to anoint Him with her precious perfume. How can her story help shape our attitudes about coming to Christ?

1. She came prepared
2. She humbled herself
3. She honored Jesus
4. She wept – I believe tears of repentance
5. She received salvation
6. She left forever changed

Are you heavy-hearted today? Do you think it is too late for you? Do you have a family member or a friend whose life is a mess? Reach out to Jesus. I guarantee you He is waiting. Humble yourself in His presence, and you will be forever changed. Find your hope at the feet of Jesus.

Hope for Daily Living

Alabaster jars were carved, expensive, and beautiful yet this never-named woman was willing to break it open and pour its expensive contents over the feet of Jesus. Do you have something you have been holding onto; afraid to relinquish to Christ? Perhaps it is a possession, a person, or an emotion. Are you willing to pour it out at His feet today? Explain.

Read Luke 8:16-17. The never-named woman publicly displayed her adoration for Jesus by braving a room filled with men who felt she did not belong. Are you willing to unashamedly shine your light for Christ? If so, how?

Remember, our never-named woman came to the feet of Christ that day, prepared, humbled, and in tears. Because she hoped enough to display her faith, she left forever changed. Have you had that experience with Jesus? Has your life been forever changed? If not, are you ready and willing to meet Him right now? If you are, there are Scriptures to help you on page 223.

Heavenly Father, in the precious Name of Jesus, I come today. I lay my family, possessions, emotions, and attitudes at the feet of Jesus. I ask you to forgive me of sin in my life, clarify your calling on my life, and restore lost hope so that I am able to light up my world with the light of the truth about Jesus. Please, place opportunities in my path, and give me the wisdom and courage to shine your light that unbelievers might come to recognize and know that You are God. Lord, I carry hope in my heart, ready to pour it out like the never-named woman with her alabaster jar at the feet of Jesus. In His precious name I pray. Amen and Amen!

Chapter Seventeen

Hope

During Times

Of Trouble

But you, God,

see the trouble of the afflicted;

you consider their grief

and take it in hand.

Psalm 10:14a

Recently, across our nation, wicked acts have piled one on top of another at an alarming rate. The number of police officers shot and killed or injured in the line of duty is staggering. Parents grieve their lost children. Wives wonder how they will raise their sons and daughters. Brothers and sisters sob in disbelief. Many might ask, where is God? Why do the wicked succeed? Does God even care? Where is our hope during times of trouble?

During times of trials and heartaches, a walk through the Psalms can tell us much about the heart of God. Psalm 10:14 describes God's actions. "But you, O God, do see…" God looks, views, considers, and realizes what is happening. This verse tells us He sees the "trouble of the afflicted…" He sees our work, labor, toil, misery and oppression. He sees the wrong, abuse, distress, and suffering. He sees and understands what is happening to the humble, afflicted, poor, helpless, and needy.

So, how do we reconcile the goodness of God versus the evil of man? Does God only see? Psalm 10:14 makes it clear that God sees and acts when the writer tells us, "You (*God*) consider it, to take it in hand." In the original Hebrew, the word in this verse translated *consider* can also mean have regard for, tolerate, detect, observe, watch over, and esteem. God observes and considers the acts of evil, trouble, grief… Why? Verse fourteen tells us, "to take it in hand." And there is our hope! The hand of God.

The Hebrew word for *hand* used here is yād; control, power, strength, direction, or care. Not only does God see the outward circumstances and know the inward feelings caused by the evil we face, He has the power to control the situation, provide strength in the midst of trouble, give direction, and care for His children along the journey.

While we may not understand God's timetable, it is important to remember that God judges sin. Verse sixteen tells us He is King. Throughout the Psalms we find many images of God. He is:

Our Shield
Our Rock
Our King
Our Shepherd
Our Judge
Our Refuge
Our Fortress
Our Avenger
Our Creator
Our Deliverer
Our Healer
Our Protector

Our Provider
Our Redeemer

Do not let the evils of this world cause you to doubt
that God still cares for His children, on His
timeline, in His way. Just as He delivered the
Hebrew children from the clutches of Egypt, He is
able to come to our aide in times of distress; our
hope during times of trouble.

Hope for Daily Living

Do you ever doubt that God is in control of earth's
events? Yes or no, and explain.

From the list above, which image of God is most
relevant to your needs at this time? Why?

Read Psalm 91. Write verses 1-2 here.

Read Psalm 93. What do these verses tell you about God?

In your own words, write a prayer of praise and thanksgiving.

Father, You know that our world is a mess, and satan would like nothing more than to have us dwell on the evil and sadness that can be found in this life. But You, O God, are Light in the darkness, Strength in my weakness, Refuge in my storms, a Shield in my battles, Provider in my times of need, Healer in my times of illness, my Rock to stand on when I feel I am sinking, my Deliverer from the enemy, and my Redeemer for eternity. Praise Your Holy Name! In the Name of Jesus, I thank You that You are my hope during times of trouble. Amen.

Hope through God's Preparation

Since I was very young, I somehow had a "feeling" that there was a plan for my life...even though some days, I didn't know if I would live to see another.

I was abused (physically and mentally) by my parents as early as age 3, and it continued until I got married at 18. During the times of abuse, I felt I was going through it alone, but I was not alone.

At 8 or 9 I started going to church with other family members and read the Bible almost through looking for that hope I knew was there. As a teenager I committed my life to Christ and was at church every opportunity; my escape to my hope of a different climate because my home life was not stable or supportive.

I married early, trying to create my own hope, in my own way. But, after ten plus years of a bad marriage, I was once again on the journey for this hope and recommitted my life to Christ.

He has been faithful to me while I have been on my journey for hope. Through all of this, I have learned the only hope I have in this life is through Him. My hope and my salvation are in the Lord.

I believe that I am now on the right path—God's path instead of my own. He has been so faithful to me through it all. As I do the work He placed in my heart to do for Him, I hope one day to hear those words, "Well done, my good and faithful servant."

—Marie
Michigan

Chapter Eighteen

Hope

Replaces

Condemnation

Therefore, there is now

no condemnation

for those

who are in

Christ Jesus.

Romans 8:1

Condemnation comes in many forms; criticism, disapproval, rebuke, judgment… Our world today seems filled with those who easily find fault in others; condemning you for your beliefs, words, or actions with no thought as to how their criticism and negative words might change the course of your life.

But, have you considered that you may be your own worst enemy when it comes to condemnation? Most likely you have heard the phrase "jack of all trades—master of none." Those are the words that satan whispered in my ears for decades. Every time I heard a great pianist perform, an accomplished singer sing, read a fine work of literature, or saw a remarkable photograph displayed, my mind would rush to the "if only I had" focused on one thing: piano, vocal, composition, photography—"then I would not be a…jack of all trades and master of none." Heaping condemnation upon myself became a bad habit.

Perhaps you too have played the self-condemnation game. But Romans 8:1 says "there is now no condemnation for those who are in Christ Jesus." While we usually think of this verse in the context of freedom from sin by the redeeming blood of Jesus Christ, I would like you to think outside the box for a moment. 1 John 3:19-21 tells us that God is greater than your conscience, your thought process, or the rationalization of your behavior.

Psalm 139 beautifully proclaims God's activity in your life before your lungs inhaled for the first time. Almighty God looked upon you while you grew in your mother's womb. Verses fifteen and sixteen explain that before your body was formed, all the days God ordained for you were written in His book; before a single one of them came to be.

God loves you, and you are so precious to Him that rather than condemn you, when you were an embryo, in a little tight ball, He planned your days and wrote them down in His book. That does not mean we will never face trials, temptations, or sorrows but that as soon as you surrender your life to the Father through Jesus Christ His Son, you are in safe hands; no longer condemned. Sin cannot condemn you, satan cannot condemn you, and you cannot condemn yourself.

Never again allow satan to whisper, "You are not good enough," in your ear. Never again allow him to convince you that you have sinned too often, been too bad, or done too much wrong to be useful in God's Kingdom. Never again allow satan to make you believe that you are "just ok" in your service for the Father, because 1 Peter 5:8 tells us that our "enemy the devil prowls around like a roaring lion looking for someone to devour."

Do not let it be you! Find hope in the words Jesus spoke to a woman caught in the act of adultery in John 8:11b, "And Jesus said unto her, 'Neither do I condemn thee go, and sin no more.'" (KJV) Let hope replace condemnation in your life.

Hope for Daily Living

Do you have a tendency toward self-condemnation? If so, in what area of your life?

Read 1 John 3:19-21. Is there a particular word or phrase that catches your attention in these verses? Explain.

Read Psalm 139 then write the words of Hope you find.

If you desire to never again allow satan to devour your witness for Christ, your testimony to the goodness of God, or your ability to faithfully serve God in any area He chooses for you, write your commitment here.

Never forget: Hope Replaces Condemnation!

Heavenly Father, Help me remember that in Christ I am forgiven, rescued, redeemed, chosen, justified, accepted, alive, loved, free, and taken care of. You meet every need. You fulfill every promise. You prepare the way for me to follow your calling. You never forget me, and the hope I find in You replaces all condemnation. Thank You for loving me. Here I am, Lord. In the precious Name of Jesus, send me! Amen.

Chapter Nineteen

Hope

in the Midst

of Pain.

He will wipe every

tear from their eyes.

There will be no more death

or mourning

or crying

or pain.

Revelation 21:4a

Several days ago, something bit my foot underneath my big toe. In the morning, I walked without effort, but by late afternoon, the pain made it impossible to place my foot on the floor. The next day my foot was red, swollen, and my ankle puffed up like a pin cushion. I don't like going to the doctor, but I realized without overnight improvement I would have no option. Before going to bed, I prayed for healing.

Finally, I dozed off to sleep fully expecting a trip to the doctor would consume my next morning. But, when I awakened, I could tell there was some change for the better. So, I waited. Over the last week, my foot has improved a little each day. I'm in flip flops and able to place the full weight of my body on my foot; a little redness and soreness remains. Healing is almost complete.

Moments spent sitting with my foot elevated gave me time to think about the kinds of pain that cover our world. Satan would like to use that pain to shroud your world and mine in hopelessness. Pain scatters through the body like a farmer scatters feed in a chicken coup. It goes everywhere. And when no relief is found, physical pain can become emotional pain—emotional pain can become physical pain.

The pain of long-term or terminal illness can result in mental anguish, distress, misery, anxiety, worry, and grief. The pain of lost friendship or broken relationship might cause you to build a wall around your heart in hope that no one will ever be able to hurt you again. The pain of missing out on an opportunity you prayed and hoped for might cause you to give up, stop trying, or decide you will never accomplish your goals.

Pain is real. Pain can be hurtful or excruciating; uncomfortable or grievous; stinging or searing. Pain hurts!

But, in some instances, pain brings hope and healing. An arm pain might cause you to see your doctor in time to discover a serious heart condition. Stomach pain might lead to the discovery of a tumor in time to save your life. The pain of grief may lead you into a more intimate relationship with The Almighty.

Your ultimate hope of freedom from pain will come as you drop the chains from your earth-bound body and your spirit rises to forever be with the Lord. But here and now, on planet earth, you have this hope:

2 Corinthians 4:16-18 "Therefore we do not lose
heart.
Though outwardly we are wasting away, yet
inwardly
we are being renewed day by day. For our light
and momentary troubles are achieving for
us an eternal glory that far outweighs
them all. So we fix our eyes
not on what is seen,
but on what is unseen.
For what is seen
is temporary,
but
what
is
unseen
is
eternal."

When instinct invites you to flee trials, to give in to
temptation, or to give up in despair, *REMEMBER*
even when you are right in the middle of pain and
suffering, God's will is working in you.

Romans 8:17-18 Now if we are children, then we
are
heirs—heirs of God and co-heirs with Christ, if
indeed
we share in his sufferings in order that we may also
share in his glory. I consider that
our present sufferings are not
worth comparing
with the glory
that will
Be revealed in us."

Never forget:

Psalm 147:3 He heals
The brokenhearted
and
binds up
their
wounds.

There is hope in the midst of pain. "Christ in you,
the hope of glory." (Colossians 1:27b)

Hope for Daily Living

Are you presently enduring some physical and/or emotional pain?

Have you lost heart, or are you on the verge of just giving up? If so, why?

Write 1 Peter 5:9-10.

Read Psalm 50:15, Nahum 1:7, Psalm 6:2, Psalm 68:19. Write your praise to God here.

Heavenly Father, You are my comfort in my sufferings because Your promise preserves my life. Your Word gives me patience and encouragement so that I can have hope in the midst of good times and bad times. I know You will work all things together for good. Forgive me during times of doubt and confusion. I know you are Almighty God who delivers and rescues Your children. Thank you for being my hope in the midst of pain. In the precious Name of Jesus Christ my Savior. Amen and Amen.

Chapter Twenty

Dare

to

Hope

Even if I thought

there was

still

hope

for me

Ruth 1:12

Love hopes all things (1 Cor. 13:7); Christ in you, the hope of glory (Col. 1:27); Be joyful in hope (Romans. 12:12); Hope is an anchor of the soul (Heb. 6:19); Character produces hope (Rom. 5:4).

Yes, hope is an anchor of your soul, but what happens when you lose hope? Have you been there? Have the circumstances of life dealt you such a blow that you perceived no way out of the confusion, loss, or hopelessness?

Has satan ensnared you, have friends deserted you, have you been hanging onto hope for so long that you have finally decided there is no longer any reason to hope things might change? Are you like Naomi in the biblical account of Ruth and Naomi when Naomi said, "Even if I thought there was still hope for me…?" (Ruth 1:12)

Are you there? At the "even if I thought…" What do you do with that? Where do you find the courage to dare to hope again?

Be encouraged! God sees you in your circumstances. You can neither flee from God nor find a place to hide where He is not with you. Psalm 139 reveals that God knows when you come and go, when you sit or rise, and what you will say before words exit your mouth. You are not alone.

There is always a reason to hope. If you do not believe that, flip the pages of your Bible over to John 3:16 and remember God loves you so much He sent His One and Only Son to give His life in exchange for your sin that you might have eternal life. You are loved!

Refuse to let circumstances or satan keep you bound by hopelessness. Believe God. Dare to hope!

Hope for Daily Living

Read 1 Corinthians 13:7, Colossians 1:27, Romans 12:12, Hebrews 6:19, and Romans 5:4, and write the words that detail the reason you can dare to hope during times of adversity.

Read Psalm 139. Write the words or passages that remind you that you can dare to hope.

129

Read John 3:16. Write it here as a reminder of the reason for your hope.

Father in heaven, I give You praise and thank You for Your Son Jesus who is the reason for my hope. He is the joy, the anchor, the security and the always steadfast incomprehensible hope that no matter where I am in life or what I am experiencing I can dare to hope. Thank You, Father, for Your deep, profound, complete, unimaginable love for me. Thank You for Jesus Who comes to rescue, save, and show me the Image of the Invisible God; what You look like to me. Thank you that no matter what life throws in my direction, I can dare to hope in You. In the sweet and most precious Name Above All Names, Jesus Christ my Lord. Amen and Amen.

Hope in the face of New Challenges

Granny Jones, my mom and a couple other ladies from the church decided to go to driver's education together. I don't know how old granny Jones was but my mom was in her late 50s.

Granny Jones passed her written test and a young officer took her out for her driving test. Close to the end of the test, she jumped a curb and ran into a tree. The officer got out, checked her car and told her she could back up.

When she got back on the street, he told her to go ahead and drive back to the police station and he would meet her there and process her license. She asked if he wasn't going to go back with her, and he said it was a nice day and he was just going to walk back.

That's how I recall my mom telling the

story. But there's another story in all this.

When my mom decided she was ready to go take her driver's test, she asked if I would take her because she didn't want dad there! I took her and had to drive around the police station several times trying to find a spot where she could just pull out of the parking space and not have to back up.

I finally found one and when she left with the officer, I went to the top floor and watched. She got in the car, got situated, started it and proceeded to back into the car behind her!!!! No damage was done so the officer had her continue her test.

When we were ready to leave with her license in hand, she asked if I saw what happened. I admitted I had and she looked at me and said, "If you ever tell *your dad or brother, I'll kill you!" I lost it! I knew my mom would not have killed me; but, I kept her secret...until she left this life to go be with her Heavenly Father.*

Shortly after her death, my dad, brother, husband and I stood around her body in the family room of the ER and shared moments in her life. I shared the story above with them and, again, we all lost it - lost it so bad the doctor and nurse came back into the room to console us only to find us with smiles on our face and tears streaming down our cheeks.

—Ina
California

Chapter Twenty-One

Abiding

Hope

"I am the vine,

you are the branches;

he who abides in Me and I in him,

he bears much fruit,

for apart from Me you can do nothing.

John 15:5 NASB

As a girl, I loved going to my grandparent's house for many reasons including my cousins who lived next door, and my grandparent's garden which provided a huge playground and, in the summer months, a luscious snack area. The regular Sunday drive from our home to theirs offered time for me to hope for something delicious to be ready to harvest.

Grandpa's Concord grapes grew behind the house at the front edge of the garden, providing me with shelter from prying eyes as I ate my fill. The deep rich purple skin and the beautiful spreading vines often drew my attention away from my surroundings as I became lost in the sugary treat. I quickly learned to pull the grapes one by one from the hanging bunches rather than breaking a piece of the vine because the life of the fruit is dependent upon the vine.

That lesson has served me well throughout my spiritual journey. From childhood until now, my desire to be fruitful in God's Kingdom has depended upon my ability to stay connected to the *true vine.* Just like a grape with no nourishment, when I allow busyness to isolate me from the *vine*, my spiritual desire to be fruitful shrivels.

Have you found that to be true? Do you sometimes allow the burdens and busyness of life to interrupt your relationship with the life-giving nourishment of the *true vine*?

John 15:5 explains the principle needed to bear much fruit in your spiritual journey. Christ is the *vine*, and you are the branch. In order to bear those beautiful bunches of fruit, you must abide in the vine; Christ. Remain in Him. Live in Him. Dwell in Him. Endure with Him. Keep on keeping on with Him. Because, Jesus says in John 15:5, "…apart from me you can do nothing." No Thing! By yourself, separately, without, or independent from Christ—you and I can do No Thing!

Unlike the grape on the grapevine, spiritual fruit comes in a diverse display of abiding in the *vine*. Making Christ Savior and Lord. Obedience to the Father. Answered prayer. Love. Joy. Peace. Patience. Kindness. Goodness. Faithfulness. Gentleness. Self-Control. Soul-Winning; and more…

Therefore, staying connected to Christ is essential to living a life of abiding hope. A life that bears much fruit. A life filled with joy in the midst of pain. A life filled with peace in the midst of persecution. A life filled with expectancy in the midst of sorrow. A life filled with promise in the midst of disappointment. A life filled with purpose in the midst of defeat.

Working in a job you do not like, raising small children, raising teenagers, putting a life goal on hold, caring for an aging parent or an ailing spouse, or a hundred other circumstances can consume your time and keep you from abiding in the *vine*. But abiding hope comes when you remain in, endure, and keep on receiving the nourishment found only in remaining in Christ.

Let today be the day you make a commitment to be the branch that never shrivels as you realize abiding hope.

Hope for Daily Living

Write John 15:5. Write your personal definition of abiding hope.

Read John 15:1-4. Is there anything in your life that you need to allow the Father, as gardener, to prune? If so, write it here and make a commitment to discuss it with the Father.

If you do not already have a daily specific time set aside with the Father, are you willing to make a commitment to begin today? You can start with five minutes and lengthen the time as you desire

Write YES below if you are willing to memorize John 15:5. This will help you keep it in the forefront of your mind on those difficult days when there seems to be no time for God!

Heavenly Father, today I desire a more intimate relationship with you; a relationship that initiates abiding hope in my life. Hope that endures through every circumstance. Hope that is based completely on being the branch that never becomes severed from the vine. Hope that permeates my life and the lives of those around me. Please allow me the joy and privilege of bearing much fruit for You. Thank you for patiently pruning me. In the most precious Name of Jesus. Amen.

Hope

When Life Hangs in the Balance

December 6, 1993; my day was to start off with a doctor's appointment. I had been diagnosed with severe preëclampsia and was going weekly to be monitored. My husband was in the Air Force and our plan was for me to deliver our baby at Eglin Air Force Base. Funny how sometimes our plans and God's plans don't always line up with one another isn't it?

My husband drove us to the Air Base for what we thought would be our normal weekly appointment. We were wrong! I had to go the day before (Dec. 5th) to do some lab work and the results were not good. They repeated the labs when I was at the doctor's office and placed an order to have them done STAT. They were hoping somehow a mistake had been made in the lab. However, the results came back even worse than the original labs. Somehow, my platelets were being destroyed. The doctors informed me I was going to be admitted to the hospital and have my baby. I was still almost seven weeks away from my due date.

This was my first baby, my only baby! I was scared out of my mind. It was just my husband, me, and the medical team. (I was so scared for a moment I had forgotten all about God being with me and my baby). My parents and my in-laws were over 500 miles away—in Tennessee! My husband called my mom and told her what was going on, and she asked if she could talk to me. She told me she would be praying for us and would call my friends at the church and ask them to pray as well.

Thank you momma for reminding me I was not alone. Even though she was over 500 miles away, my momma gave me strength and comfort and helped me to remember that God was with me, even when she couldn't be at that time. We had no idea that as scary as things seemed at the moment they were about to become even scarier! They got me in a room in the labor/delivery area of the hospital. An ultrasound technician came in to do an ultrasound on the baby. A few minutes later a doctor came in and informed me that the hospital wasn't going to accept my baby because the birth weight was assumed to be under seven pounds.

They informed me they were transferring me to a civilian hospital approximately thirty minutes from my home. I had never been to the hospital they transferred me to! I had never been to any doctors in Pensacola. Now I was going to have a baby delivered by people I had never even seen or heard of before? YES, scary just got even scarier!

The doctors started to induce my labor at the Air Base hospital and when I arrived at Sacred Heart Hospital they continued with the Pitocin drip. After several hours, the doctors spoke to me about a possible C-section. First they wanted to break my water to see if that would help my labor along. They had already ordered six units of blood and six units of platelets to be on standby due to my platelets being destroyed.

The doctor's broke my water and my baby had a prolapsed cord. Immediately both my blood pressure and heart rate and the baby's dropped! We were in real trouble! They quickly rushed me to surgery and performed an emergency C-section. Six short

minutes later, Miss Ambriel
Taylor Long was born at 1:36 a.m. She
weighed a little over 4 pounds and 3
ounces and was 18 1/2 inches long.
Amber was taken straight to the NICU
(Neonatal Intensive Care Unit). The
precious nurses in the NICU took a
couple of pictures of my sweet baby so
I could see what she looked like. Miss
Ambriel was two days old before I got
to see her in person. Due to
complications with her delivery, I was
kept sedated for a while. When I did
come out of the sedation, the first thing
I said was B-A-B-Y. I was asked if there
was anything they could do for me by
one of the nurses. I said, "Yes, I want to
see my baby".

When I wanted to see her (and that
was all the time), I had to go to her.
There were certain visitation hours for
the NICU as well. The walk down to
the NICU was exhausting—especially

after having major surgery, but God gave me the strength I needed to make that journey. My time was limited with my precious baby, but I understood that was for her protection as to not cause any more stress on her little body than possible.

We had certain rather rigorous routines that we had to do before seeing the baby, certain ways we had to scrub our hands and putting on gowns before entering the nursery area, not wearing any jewelry all little things that played a MAJOR role in these precious babies' health and wellbeing.

When my parents made the trip down to Florida to see their first grandbaby, of course they wanted to see her right away. Those precious nurses were awesome in allowing them to do that.

Prior to my parents meeting Amber, they got to meet a few of the doctors *that were a part of my delivery team. My dad walked up to them and introduced himself. He shook hands with them and told them he wanted to thank them for saving his daughter and his grand-daughter.*

One of the doctors told my daddy this, "Mr. Tidwell, there was a higher power involved, and it was God that saved them sir, not me. He (God) must have a special purpose for them being here. We have never got to keep both the mother and the baby in situations like your daughter's, we have always lost one of them. This was a first for us."

My parents then went to visit with their grandbaby. It was the baby's turn to be checked on. As we were walking down the various hallways to the NICU nursery, I was trying to prepare them as to what they would see in the NICU. It is a different place filled with different sounds of machines and equipment making odd noises that one would not expect in a nursery. There are no open windows for the public to gaze upon the babies—it can be overwhelming.

Parents of children in the NICU often feel ALL they have when it comes to their babies getting well is HOPE. HOPE for them to get better, HOPE for them to leave the NICU and go home, and HOPE for their children to be able to live happy and wonderful lives. Without hope, they often feel like they have nothing. HOPE is something that is very important to a parent of a baby in the NICU.

My HOPE and what I clung to was my faith in my Heavenly Father. Jeremiah 29:11 (NIV) says, "For I know the plans I have for you, declares the Lord, plans to prosper you and not to harm you, plans to give you hope and a future." What an amazing promise, a *promise that I still hold, claim, and cling to even today!*

Amber had a few concerns when she was born. She had a low birth weight, couldn't maintain her body temperature at a safe level, jaundice, and a real scary concern was she didn't know how to suck so couldn't really take a bottle without issues. Although these were serious concerns, there were infants all around her in worse condition.

I remember talking to one of the doctors in the NICU one day and I was asking if maybe Amber would be able to be home for Christmas—after just being born December 7th. This was my Christmas wish, my miracle I was praying for, HOPING for. The doctor didn't think it would be possible. She had lost some weight due to her not knowing how to suck on a bottle. However, let me tell you that with my

God *ALL* things are possible! I prayed
and gave my concerns, my wish, over
to God. Amber spent a total of 10 days
in the NICU and was discharged Dec.
17th. I got my Christmas wish!

I was told that due to being a preemie
Amber might have a low resistance
and be sick a lot. She wasn't. She would
have a cold or an earache every now
and then but no more than normal. I
was told there might be developmental
problems and even academic issues
when she went to school.

Now, fast-forward several years, my
baby girl has graduated high school
with Beta- Club honors, she is enrolled
in college and is excelling there as well
and will soon graduate. She has grown
into a beautiful Christian young lady.
She is indeed one of my most wonderful
and most precious blessings, a true gift
from God. My daughter that I prayed
for (and still pray for daily), and

HOPED for, Ambriel Taylor Long.

Thank you Father for the gift of my daughter and for choosing me, blessing me with the opportunity to be her mommy. Thank you that You are our hope when life hangs in the balance.

—Lisa
Tennessee

Chapter Twenty-two

Sacrificial

Hope

But, I with a song of thanksgiving,

will sacrifice to you.

What I have vowed

I will make good.

Salvation comes from the LORD.

Jonah 2:9

Most of us are familiar with the story of "Jonah and the Whale." As children, many of us learned that Jonah disobeyed God, jumped on a boat going in the opposite direction from the city where God commanded Jonah to preach, and was thrown overboard to save the ship from a violent storm. Then a great fish swallowed him and, after his fervent prayer to God for relief, it vomited Jonah onto dry ground.

The prophet, unwilling to fulfill the seemingly offensive mission from God, chose to run rather than obey. Ultimately, however, Jonah realized that God's way was the only way and, although he remained reluctant, he obeyed God. The people of Nineveh believed and were saved, but Jonah pouted and sulked in anger; complaining to God. He became so angry that he wanted to die. (Jonah 4:9) Jonah hated the powerful and wicked Assyrians of Nineveh.

But God, in His great mercy, saved both the Ninevites and Jonah from their own destructive choices. Initially, Jonah was unwilling to sacrifice his desires to fulfill the calling of God on his life. But, he was willing to sacrifice his life to save the sailors on the ship he chose to board while fleeing from God. His behavior seems to be a conundrum, mind-boggling, a puzzle.

As I thought about the complexity of Jonah's actions, I realized that you and I face similar dilemmas. For example, your heart's desire, your hope in life, may be to minister to the hurting in your community or nearby city. However, what if God's answer is yes to allowing you to minister to the hurting, but His call on your life is to the inner city of Mumbai, India where the population is over twelve million. Are you willing to make the sacrifice? What if your ministry desire lies across the nation but instead, God calls you across town? What if you desire to do "great things" for God *by the world's standards,* yet He calls you to a ministry of obscurity where few ever know your name? Are you willing to make that sacrifice as you hope in Him?

The twists and turns of life often lead you to unexpected places, often put you in unexpected situations, and often leave you with unexpected decisions to make. But as my favorite Psalm teaches, there is no place you can run, hide, or rest that God cannot find you. (Psalm 139) The question becomes are you, am I, willing to live with sacrificial hope; hope that seeks obedience to God rather than hope that seeks the fulfillment of a personal desire.

Sacrificial hope draws you and me to look

expectantly for God's direction. Sacrificial hope presents a grateful heart to God for the ability to present the Truth of God's Word to the hungry broken heart of a desperate lost soul. Sacrificial hope allows earthly eyes to see beyond the natural realm. Sacrificial hope is not confined to the mighty in word and deed, but rather becomes a powerful tool for God's Kingdom in the hearts of struggling single moms, those bed-ridden by illness, dads working two or three jobs, young college graduates looking for work, grandparents raising their grandchildren, soldiers on the battlefield, surgeons in the operating room, and a myriad of other life situations.

Sacrificial hope means believing and obeying God. I am glad God included Jonah's story in His Word to you and me. It is in God's Word that we are allowed to see the imperfections, rocky beginnings, and sometimes shaky endings of those who first believed God; human beings like you and like me. God's Word teaches us to repent, obey, and believe Him. From the darkness inside the belly of a great fish, Jonah cried out to God with his words of sacrificial hope, "But I, with a song of thanksgiving, will sacrifice to you. What I have vowed I will make good. Salvation comes from the LORD."

Pray with me: Father, I pray that like the Ninevites who were saved because Jonah preached and they repented, many will come to know You because of my sacrificial hope in You.

Hope for Daily Living

In chapter one of Jonah, we find him running from God. Have you ever run from God? If so, what were the circumstances?

What strengths did Jonah display in the midst of his circumstances? List them here.

What weaknesses and/or mistakes did Jonah display in the midst of his circumstances? List those here.

What lessons can you learn from Jonah's good and bad decisions?

How will those lessons impact your view of sacrificial hope?

Heavenly Father, today I sing a song of praise and thanksgiving as I think about sacrificial hope. Thank you for teaching me that obedience to your calling may cause me to set aside my hopes and dreams or obedience may bring about fulfillment of what my heart longs for. Either way, LORD, obedience brings answered prayer and blessing from you. Thank you that obedience changes my perspective from what I hope for to what You have in store for me. Your Word teaches me that while I was yet unformed in my mother's womb, you had a plan for me. Please, open my heart to be willing to allow sacrificial hope to replace my selfish desires. I ask in the precious Name of Jesus and for Your glory. Amen and Amen.

Chapter Twenty-three

Hope

To Cross

Your

Red Sea

Moses answered, the people,

"Do not be afraid.

Stand firm and you will see the deliverance

the LORD will bring you today...

The LORD will fight for you;

you need only to be still.

Exodus 14:13a, 14

Imagine with me the dilemma faced by the Israelites when, with one final plague over Egypt, God changed the world as they knew it—forever. For four hundred thirty years, to the day, (Exodus 12:40) they lived, worked, and eventually became enslaved in Egypt. Genesis 46:27 tells us that seventy direct descendants of Jacob (Israel) went into Egypt, and after four hundred thirty years, 603,550 men age twenty and older plus women, children, and the Tribe of Levi fled Egypt. In approximately twenty-four days, according to some studies I read, well over one million people camped by the Red Sea.

Exodus 14:10 tells us, "As Pharaoh approached, the Israelites looked up, and there were the Egyptians, marching after them. They were terrified and cried out to the LORD." Husbands fearful for their wives and children. Mothers fearful for their nursing babies. Children fearful of the thunderous roar of chariots and hoof beats. Then fear turned to anger as accusations against Moses and *I told you so* language could be heard throughout the desert.

When it looked like they were trapped, Moses called upon God and encouraged the people with these words, "Do not be afraid. Stand firm and you will see the deliverance the LORD will bring you today. The Egyptians you see today you will never see again. The LORD will fight for you; you need only be still." (Exodus 14:13-14) Hope to cross the Red Sea.

What happened next has been immortalized in print and film over generations. God made a dry-land path across the Red Sea. The Israelites crossed, and when Pharaoh's army followed, the sea swallowed every last Egyptian. The Israelites never saw the Egyptian army again! God always keeps His Word!

Rather than an imposing body of water before you and an army of chariots behind you, a busy schedule may pursue you from the moment your feet hit the floor in the morning until the last piece of laundry is folded, the last child stops asking for a drink of water, and the last item on your to-do list is moved to tomorrow.

Your Red Sea may be an aging parent, a wayward child, or empty-nest syndrome. Your Red Sea may be waiting for the doctor's report, the job interview results, or reconciliation with a loved one. Your Red Sea may be an empty checkbook, an empty pantry, and an empty gas tank. Your Red Sea may be a secret you have never shared while the thunder of shame and rejection beats in your ears.

Your Red Sea may be the fault of others or a creation of your own decisions. But here is the good news! God sees you. He can make a way in the desert and streams in your wasteland. (Isaiah 43:19b) God either placed you where you are or allowed circumstances to bring you to this place. Hebrews 13:6 reminds us that during times of great stress or insecurity we can say with confidence, "The Lord is my helper; I will not be afraid. What can man do to me?"

Do you feel trapped between a rushing army and a raging sea? Perhaps God is testing your faith. Perhaps He is weaving you into a beautiful masterpiece, and for now you are only allowed to see the jagged threads on the underside of the cloth. Perhaps He is preparing to open the sea and allow you to walk across on dry land.

"Do not be afraid. Stand firm and you will see the deliverance the LORD will bring you… The LORD will fight for you; you need only be still." He is Hope to cross your Red Sea.

Hope for Daily Living

Are you facing your own Red Sea experience? Explain.

Read 2 Chronicles 20:15. Write it here. Memorize it. How can this verse help you face your Red Sea battle?

Do you believe God can work wonders in your Red Sea situation? Affirm it here. Cement it in writing.

In the midst of your struggles, do not forget to praise God. Read Psalm 150, and accept this challenge: Praise God every day for thirty days and write the results here.

Heavenly Father, I praise You that You heal the brokenhearted and bind up our wounds. You are great and mighty in power. Your understanding knows no limits. You sustain the humble and bless Your people. I praise You because You alone are worthy of praise. Thank you, Father, for reminding me that You are able to blow the wind of change into my life and lead me across my Red Sea on dry ground. Thank you that while I wait to see the results of Your working in my life, I can trust that You have my best interest in mind. Remind me, Lord, there is joy in the journey as I believe You for the results. Build my faith. Hold me close. Teach me to trust You with an unfaltering faith as I wait in Hope to cross my Red Sea. Thank you, Lord, for loving me. In the most precious Name of Jesus. Amen and Amen.

Chapter Twenty-Four

Hope

In the Face of

Persecution

Who shall separate us

from the

love of Christ?

Shall trouble or hardship

or persecution...

Romans 8:35

I remember school-year's childhood bullies. They harassed, tormented, mistreated, and abused (sometimes physically but always emotionally) students they perceived as weaker than themselves. The bully pursued with intensity his seemingly helpless victim; cornering him in the hallway, surrounding him in a circle of like-minded friends on the playground, verbally abusing him, and sometimes physically picking at or attacking him until his spirit was crushed, and he was humiliated in front of all those watching. Persecuted for not acquiescing.

Our oldest and youngest son each faced a bullying situation in middle school. My husband and I taught our children to never start a fight but to defend themselves if necessary. With one son, talking with an administrator remedied the situation. However, the other son's bully went to the classroom seeking out our son and charged him like a bull after a red bandana. Our son defended himself, but both boys were taken to the principal's office, and both boys were going to be but in In-School Suspension for three days.

I vigorously objected. Our son was where he was supposed to be, doing what he was supposed to be doing, with a teacher who witnessed the actions of the bully bursting into the room for the sole purpose of attacking our son. As a mother, there was no way I was going to allow my son to be punished for simply defending himself. The principal consented; adding one statement to his ruling: "If it happens again, your son will also go to ISS."

At that moment I did what any God-fearing, Christian, loving mother would do. I turned to our son and said, "If he comes after you again, you better get three-days-worth of him because apparently you will be going to ISS for defending yourself." As the principal called my name while picking his jaw up off the desk, I smiled, said thank you for your cooperation, and we left his office. The bully spent three days in ISS with the understanding that our son was not an easy target.

In Romans 8:35, the Apostle Paul conveys how much Christ loves you and me. When faced with hardship, danger, or persecution, His love never fails. In a time when Christians are being persecuted across our country, and make no mistake, *Christians are being persecuted,* it is a blessing to read the words of Christ as written down in Matthew 5:10, "Blessed are those who are persecuted because of righteousness, for theirs is the kingdom of heaven."

Because of *righteousness*! Whose righteousness?

Romans 3:10 tells us, "There is no one righteousness, not even one." Our righteousness is only found through faith in our Heavenly Father and His Son Jesus Christ. Being in right standing with God is our righteousness. Therefore, if and when you or I are persecuted because of righteousness as indicated in Matthew 5:10, we are being persecuted because we are Christian.

So where is your hope in a world becoming more and more hostile towards Christians, true believers, those who practice faith in God through Christ in every area of life? Your hope is in the love of Christ—the One in Whom you place your trust. Nothing man can do can ever separate you from His love.

The world may stereotype you as a bitter person clinging to your "guns and religion." The world may justify their name calling: bigots, close-minded, intolerant, mean... The world may try to exempt you from civic positions such as PTA leader, City Council Representative, or media personnel. The world may try to criminalize you by suing you or your business because of your failure to cooperate with those whose views you do not hold. And unfortunately, even in our country, we have seen death blows delivered for refusing to renounce the name of Christ.

So what do you do with all of that seemingly dark, defeating, discouraging information? I'm glad you ask! God's Word has the perfect prescription for the days in which we live. Be encouraged!

Don't forget against whom you are fighting when persecution arises.

Ephesians 6:10-12 Finally be strong in the Lord and in his mighty power. Put on the full armor of God so that you can take your stand against the devil's schemes. For *our struggle is not against flesh and blood*, but against the rulers, against the authorities, against the powers of this dark world and against the spiritual forces of evil in the heavenly realms.

Remember where your hope is found.

2 Thessalonians 16-17 May our *Lord Jesus Christ* himself and *God our Father*, who loved us and by his grace <u>gave us eternal encouragement and good hope</u>, encourage your hearts and strengthen you in every good deed and word.

Follow those principles, and let the enemy know that you are not an easy target. And remember, nothing, no one, no circumstance can ever separate you from the love of Christ. He is our hope in the face of persecution.

Hope for Daily Living

Have you ever encountered a bully? How did you feel? How did you react?

Do you believe that you are an easy target for persecution? Why or why not?

Read Ephesians 6:10-18. Who is our battle really against in this life?

Write Romans 8:35 and Ephesians 6:10-18 below.

When you face persecution, what will you do?

Heavenly Father, help me remember that my battles in this life are not against people. My enemy is satan. He is sly and knows how to put a human face on his personal attacks against me. When I am tempted to forget, remind me that nothing can separate me from Your love. When I am tempted to give in, remind me to put on the full armor of God and stand firm against the enemy. When I am tempted to give up, remind me that I am called to obey, and You are in total control of the consequences. Increase my faith and confidence in You, O Lord. In Jesus precious Name. Amen.

Chapter Twenty-five

Hope

In the Face of

Grief

...We do not want you

to be ignorant

about those who fall asleep,

or to grieve

like the rest of men,

who have no hope.

1 Thessalonians 4:13

Two years ago, my baby sister closed her eyes to the pain of earth and woke up to see the glories of heaven. The cares of this world fell like shackles unlocked and released from a prisoner's leg. The momentary sting of death delivered her into the arms of Jesus. Since then I have faced the loss of a nephew, my brother, an aunt, a cousin and a precious sister-in-law. Some losses were sudden and unexpected; others came after long battles with poor health.

I have learned well many lessons taught by loss. In the days following the death of my sister, grief dragged me into a pit of depression; giving me no opportunity to breathe without pain as unexpected tears marked a path from swollen eyes to my chin. Darkness hung over my heart trying to convince me I would never again see light. But slowly, shafts of light permeated the darkness and bad days gave way to okay days and finally good days.

You probably have your own such story to tell. Times of unbearable loss. Times when the darkness of grief swallowed you in its pit. Times when well-meaning words of comfort from friends rang hollow like an iron bell in an empty room. You may right now be grieving; wondering if the pain will ever end. Struggling to get out of bed. Laboring to place one foot in front of the other. There is hope.

There are many kinds of loss that can bring about grief, and while death is the focus of the Apostle Paul in 1 Thessalonians, the pain and grief caused by other losses can prove to be as debilitating as the grief of death. Loss of a friendship, financial security, physical ability, good health, a relationship breakup, etc. may cause symptoms of fear, anxiety, depression, or sleeplessness. There is hope.

I can tell you from personal experience that hope is in the Name of Jesus. During the darkest hours of my depression, I did not read the Bible; I did not pray and ask God to deliver me. I could not. You may now find yourself or a loved one in that place. But God caused His Holy Spirit to well up inside me like a spring of living water, and I began to whisper the Name of Jesus. Step one, whisper Jesus. Step two, whisper Jesus. Step three, whisper Jesus; until finally God's undeserved, unmerited, unearned, favor—grace—became a ladder of freedom from the bottom of the pit.

The Apostle Paul tells us we should not grieve like those who have no hope; those without Christ. Why? Because the resurrection of Christ brings hope. How do we have hope in times of distress? Romans 15:13 explains, "May the *God of hope* fill you with all joy and peace as you *trust in him*, so that you may *overflow with hope* by the *power of the Holy Spirit*."

Unlike our English word for hope which allows for some uncertainty, the Biblical hope as found in Ephesians 1:18 allows us to know that in Christ we have complete assurance of indisputable, unequivocal, certain victory through God. "I pray also that the eyes of your heart may be enlightened in order that you may *know the hope* to which he has called you…"

So, whatever your circumstance today, whatever has caused your grief, your pain, depression, anxiety, or hopelessness, remember that you do not need to grieve as those who have no hope. If you are overwhelmed and without the energy needed to pick up your Bible, whisper Jesus. If you find it impossible to voice a prayer, whisper Jesus. If you are struggling to put one foot in front of the other, whisper Jesus. He will come. See God in His Glory, His Majesty, His Power, His Love, and His Grace.

Trust Christ, and do not grieve as those who have no hope.

Hope for Daily Living

In what, or whom, are you placing your hope for the

future?

Do you believe God is interested in you? Why or why not?

Read Psalm 42:11, then write it here.

Read Romans 15:13 then describe what "overflow with hope" means for you.

Christians sometimes feel it is wrong to seek a counselor in times of grief or depression. Never be afraid or embarrassed to seek godly professional counseling during your time of grief.

Heavenly Father, I do not doubt that you know well the pain of grief. For as Your Son died for my sin, He was spiritually separated from You. The sun refused to shine. Darkness covered the earth as it must have mourned for the Messiah. Thank you for reminding me that You are near and You know the pain of grief, sorrow, depression, anxiety, sadness… Thank you that in the middle of life's chaos I can whisper the Name of Jesus Who brings hope and peace and renewed strength. Thank you for Your Living Word and the reminder that I can do all things through Christ who gives me strength. Thank you that when the enemy would drag me down never to rise again, You rescue, ransom, and redeem my life from the pit. My hope is in You and You alone. Thank you in the precious Name of Jesus.

Hope in Times of Grief and Loss

When Bill and I got married, we almost immediately wanted to have a child and we couldn't. Nothing we did, nothing the doctors did, could help us. So when I finally got pregnant, we felt like God had given us something special. In fact, at Christmas time, I would tie a gift tag on Terry that said, "Gift from God." That is how we always felt. Terry was just a joy to our lives.

All my life I wanted to be a pilot but that wasn't a vocation for most girls out of school in '51. Terry had my passion for flying and was able to realize his dream of being a pilot. A few days after his 60th birthday he began taking flying lessons in Colorado to get his certification for mountain flying. It was his desire to be able to fly his family from Houston to their home in Estes Park, CO. Our daughter-in-law, Gail, called one afternoon and said Terry & his instructor had not made it back to Boulder as scheduled, and the aircraft company had not been able to locate them. I think it was his third lesson out of a series of four. He and his instructor had left Boulder, Colorado to fly to Steamboat Springs and were due back at the airport at 1:00 p.m. But, by 4:00 p.m. they still had not made it.

As a mother, all night as we were waiting to hear what happened, I worried about whether he was cold, scared, what kind of injuries he had, how he was hurting; all of those things all night long. Gail finally called about 3:00-4:00 o'clock in the morning and said that they had found him. Before she could say anything else she said "and what we feared" and I said, "He's dead" and she said, "Yes." After all my worry about injuries, cold, pain, the authorities said they were killed on impact.

All through the time we were waiting for his body to be brought back to Houston, through the funeral, and everything that happened the only thing I could think of was thank you God for giving him to us.

My husband, Bill, couldn't get it through his head what had happened because he had Alzheimer's, and so I would try to explain it to him. Then he would think of something and say, "We have to call Terry," and I would have to explain it to him again. That made it really difficult to deal with; to help Bill understand that we had lost Terry. Four months later, I lost Bill as he succumbed to Congestive Heart Failure and Alzheimer's.

When I lost Bill, I was afraid that I would be fearful; anxious. But to this day I can testify I have not had fear, or been anxious for anything. I don't worry about anything. I know I am taken care of. That's a blessed gift. I hear people all the time talking about worry. In Sunday School not long ago our teacher said, "There is none of us that does not worry, right." I said, "Wrong." I do not worry anymore. I'm not anxious, I don't have to make sure my doors are locked and alarm set. I don't worry about money. I just know that God is taking care of me.

The grief is still there. I went through a good year of shock and did not even remember how I got home from Houston (a three hour drive). Recently, I asked Gail how I got home and she told me I drove myself and did not want anyone at the house when I got home. It is all a dream. I don't recall it, and I think that is another gift from God—the numbness—that you don't feel the pain.

There was so much pain between the loss of Terry and then the loss of Bill.

Bill died so peacefully. I told Linda, Gail's sister, I needed to run downstairs, and I barely walked out of the room when I'm told he gave a little shake and was gone. It was almost like he waited until I left the room—he went very peacefully.

The most wonderful thing God has done for me through this started decades ago. Bill worked for Gulf Oil and in the 1980's Chevron bought out Gulf. I had always thought that I had really strong faith and felt like I could stand up to anything. But, when we found ourselves in a position of being about five years too young to retire and not knowing what kind of security financially we would have, I was like a mad dog.

I would get up in the middle of the night and just go in circles in the living room; wringing my hands—worrying, fretting about how we were going to get by. Finally I began posting God's promises all over the house—bathroom, bedroom, living room, kitchen. I truly believe that was all that kept me sane. Bill was offered a job by an Independent Oil Company and worked for them a couple of years prior to retirement. We were amazed at how God had provided for us.

We lost an enormous amount of money on the sale of our house because of the downturn of the oil business, but we had exactly enough to pay cash for our current home. It was just provided by God. We didn't know what we were going to do, but God provided for us!

One funny thing happened. When Bill died, he was laying on our granddaughter's Minnie Mouse pillowcase. It was so funny to have all that pink under his head; Minnie Mouse instead of Mickey Mouse. I did not know ahead of time, but came to realize the casket that I chose had a drawer in it. So I wrote him a love letter, and we took the Minnie Mouse pillowcase, folded it, and put them in the drawer.

Even in the midst of great grief and loss, God has provided all that I need, and I will forever praise His name. He is our hope, our strength and comforter.

—Wanda
Texas

Chapter Twenty-six

Hope

In the Face of

Anxiety

Do not be anxious about anything,

but in everything,

by prayer and petition,

with thanksgiving,

present your requests to God.

And the peace of God,

which transcends all understanding,

will guard your hearts and your minds

in Christ Jesus.

Philippians 4:6-7

Early this morning my husband and I received an urgent phone call from our son. "I need you to pray NOW, Mom." My heart sank as I put the phone on speaker so his dad could hear. Police. Student. Accusation. Information. Our children. The longer he spoke, the more anxious I became. He and a team of adults, students, and our grandchildren held a kid's camp for a church several states away and were ready to start home when the trouble arose. "Please call your prayer warriors, gotta go, call later, bye!"

My husband and I immediately prayed then began petitioning others to pray urgently for God's intervention. After an extremely long hour—it felt like three—and acknowledgement from a myriad of pray-ers confirming their petitions to God on behalf of the mission team, our son sent a text informing us they would soon start home although the situation was not yet fully resolved.

After praising and thanking God for His speedy answer and blessing, extending my gratitude to all who prayed, and deep breathing for a few moments, I sat down to write. My title and Scripture for this chapter, chosen weeks ago, reminded me once again of God's perfect timing. There is *Hope in the Face of Anxiety.*

The Apostle Paul began Philippians 4:6 with these words, "Do not be anxious about anything…" I cannot honestly tell you that I earned an A on that portion of the test today. I definitely exhibited signs of concern and anxiety. But praise God for the remainder of that verse, "but in everything, by prayer and petition, with thanksgiving, present your requests to God."

Can you imagine the seemingly impossible task of never being anxious about anything? So, what do we do with our anxious moments—times of stress—legitimate concerns?

- Pray—Petition God. Ask for help.
- Be Thankful
- Praise God

Turn your worry into prayer. Worry Less—Pray More! When you "present your requests to God," be specific. Yes, He already knows, but remember the words of Jesus in Matthew 7:7, "Ask and it will be given to you, seek and you will find; knock and the door will be opened to you." Be persistent in your pursuit of God. Do not give up. He is not running from you. Psalm 139 tells us there is no place we can go where God is not already there. When anxiety makes your stomach roll and your knees weak, run to God not from Him.

What will happen when you do that? Philippians 4:7 says, "And the peace of God, which transcends all understanding, will guard your hearts and your minds in Christ Jesus." That is your hope in times of anxiety. God's peace guarding your heart and mind! Shielding your heart from the enemy.

We have lots of cattle ranches in Texas. As you drive along the highways, you often find areas where there is no fence across a driveway to keep the cattle inside the ranch, but rather a series of metal tubes spaced a few inches apart and buried in the ground with only the top of the tubes showing. Cattle will not cross the cattle guards. I like to think of God's peace doing the same thing for your heart and mine. Peace places a protective guard around your heart making it more difficult for satan's fiery darts to penetrate.

So, the next time you face anxiety, remember the HOPE! Present your requests to God and allow His peace that—exceeds, surpasses, goes beyond—transcends all understanding to "guard your hearts and your minds in Christ Jesus." He is your hope in the face of anxiety.

Hope for Daily Living

Describe a time when you grappled with anxiety.

Write Philippians 4:4-7.

How is God's peace different from the world's peace?

What does it mean that the "peace of God will guard your hearts and minds…"

Heavenly Father, this world is filled with things that bring anxious thoughts, anxious hearts, and troubled minds. Forgive me when I forget to allow your peace to flood over me and guard my heart and mind. When anxiety begins its work in me, remind me that You offer peace of heart and mind that is beyond human comprehension—yet attainable as I put my trust, my faith, and my hope in You alone. I pray the work I allow You to do in me during times of anxiety will bring encouragement to those in my sphere of influence and honor and glory to You and You alone. In the most precious Name of Jesus. Amen and Amen.

Hope in Times of Great Anxiety

Stepping out of the house with a sinking heart, numb mind, and eyes welling with tears, I began striding the quarter mile to the broad, grassy trail along Moses Bayou. I often run the mile long stretch with our dog, and when in most desperate need to speak with God, I make a beeline for the quietness there.

Our daughter, a college junior and beautiful Christian woman who loves her Savior was suddenly facing some serious issues. Near debilitating anxiety, depression, and panic attacks had struck her without warning. She was studying abroad for the semester and now even had a desire to no longer live. Mike and I had just gotten off the phone with her. She had been drinking. On top of these things, she had revealed something else that drove the final dagger into my heart. I couldn't walk fast enough to that place of nature in order to fall face down before God and pour out my heart and soul.

Allow me to pause here and tell you about the different types of Christians who have blessed my life. These are people to whom I can turn, and through whom the Lord can work, in varying degrees, to bring me strength, courage and peace during difficult times. I have placed these Christians into three categories...

The holies are those that sincerely strive to follow Christ and the Scriptures in order to bring God glory, as is written in 1 Peter 1:15: "...be holy in all you do..." They are disciples. They are real blessings and close friends. I consider them to be closest to the Lord in spirit, actions, and lifestyle. I love the fellowship we experience with these people.

The religious are mainly my family members, who happen to belong to a church faith that emphasizes rules and tradition. They do want to please God, they do pray, and they are mainly driven by expectations of their church doctrine. They are Pharisees – in the sense of pursuing righteousness and good deeds. I believe they care about me, and they assure me that they will pray when I'm in need. They are not as close to me as my holy friends, and seem to offer help or concern at their convenience.

The undesirables are...well, my brother-in-law, Doyle. He is a classic red neck and although a born again Christian, he is as imperfect as they come. He hunts deer and has been known to poach. He is prone to a temper (usually not toward family) with no filter for what comes out of his mouth. His crude humor often includes whatever foul reference you can imagine. He does not attend church because he doesn't trust the "plastic" people there. He hasn't always been the best father or husband. He has a history of jail terms and drug possession (not in recent years), and struggles with pain killer addiction.

Doyle is what you'd call a mess. He often does talk about the Lord and he references Scripture, causing Mike and me to privately judge him: there's no scriptural fruit here, and Doyle is certainly not a picture of Christ. He offers explanation, something we call his "big excuse", for his lowly condition with, "I'm just a sinner saved by Grace; God's work in progress". It often makes us mad!

But...Doyle would give his life for my children. I am certain; quite literally! He has a huge love. He is genuine and *extremely generous. When he says he will pray, he will. He will pray for my family members whom he may not even know or even like. And then he will ask about them weeks later. He is an encourager, a hugger and has the ability to speak gently. I consider Doyle to "be there" for me and my family much more so than any of my own blood-related family, with the exception of my mother. I am closer to him than to my own siblings. Doyle would give anything to be of help. And Mike or I have sought him often when in need of prayer or emotional support. Doyle is the real thing.*

Back at Moses Bayou, with a breaking heart, I poured out my distress to God over my precious daughter. I cried forcefully and for so long that I felt dizzy and clean out of tears. I was shocked and confused at what was happening with her; she previously seemed so happy and eager to serve God with her life. Now she was overcome by mental darkness, confusion, and doubt. She was not acting like herself and I had trouble reconciling with the fact that she was our daughter. There was a hopelessness surrounding me, a deep disappointment, guilt over the past, fear, and now my own deep depression. I longed for the presence of Jesus, but felt nothing. There were no words from Him, and no sense of His nearness. Was He here? Was He hearing?

With nothing left but a throbbing head, I trudged back home. That was it. Time to make dinner. Emptiness replaced my despair. What a waste my efforts were to connect with God back at the bayou. I was drained. What will happen now? Then my eyes caught a text message on my phone. It appeared to be from Doyle. He rarely texts me. He usually texts both Mike and me, and it is often regarding something mundane or humorous. But there in my hands was his text: "Jeanne, I don't know why, but God just laid you on my heart. I am praying for you. I'm praying for Him to wrap you in His protection." Chills overtook me as my aching eyes stared at those words. God heard me! He HEARD and was TELLING me so!

God used Doyle. None of my holy friends sent me that text. I would've surely expected something like this to come from one of these beloved disciples. As loving as they are, He didn't choose one of them. And He chose none of the religious family members.

What did all this mean to me? Firstly, I will never judge my brother-in-law again! He may just be a better picture of Christ than I am. And I can tell you through this experience to never underestimate how God can and will use the undesirables! These are the tax collectors and prostitutes. They struggle with sin, but they have a heart for God.

And secondly, God DOES hear my prayers. He IS near. And ...God DOES HEAR YOU!!!

—Jeanne
Texas

Chapter Twenty-seven

Hope

In the Face of

Loneliness

Turn to me

and be

gracious to me,

for I am

lonely and afflicted.

Psalm 25:16

Earlier, as I sat down to write, I heard a terrible squawking coming from our back deck. I immediately recognized the sound—a baby bird caught by a kitty. I rushed to the door. One yellow and white kitten and one baby male cardinal, just testing his wings, wrestled as several kittens looked on. I rescued the bird hoping he would survive. After several attempts to save him from certain death, the trauma became too much for him. I did not see any physical wounds. I think his little heart just gave out from the struggle.

Although I understand that it is critters doing what comes naturally, it always reminds me that too often people are treated like that poor cardinal. Picked on. Harassed. Afflicted. Left alone to survive the traumas foisted upon them by life's circumstances; allowing loneliness to creep in and fill the cracks and crevices of a desolate, broken heart.

King David knew something about loneliness. Chased, hunted, slandered, and distressed on many occasions—some of his wounds were self-inflicted while others grew from the jealousy and rage of those who wanted him dead. Chosen by God and anointed king as a young boy, as a man he ran for his life and hid in caves. He lived a messy life. In Psalm 25:16 we read his cry to God, "Turn to me and be gracious to me, for I am lonely and afflicted."

The thing I love about King David is that no matter the cause of the mess, his own creation or an assault from another, he always knew where to run for help. Psalm 25 begins with these words, "In you, LORD my God, I put my trust." He says it again in Psalm 86:4 and 143:8. When under attack and overwhelmed by loneliness, he knew that his hope lay in trusting God.

Loneliness arises from a myriad of situations. Friendlessness. Isolation. Estrangement. Seclusion. Companionlessness. Desertion. Abandonment. Death. These are only a few of the many causes of loneliness. You and I can be alone without being lonely—or in a crowded room and yet feel completely isolated from others.

Loneliness can happen when you feel deserted, disconnected, devoid of physical or emotional support from those you love. Emotional hurt or betrayal might cause you to withdraw from your network of family and friends, to build an imaginary wall around your heart, to determine you will never again be hurt; the beginning of an emotional downward spiral that can leave you, and those who love you, drowning in a pool of loss and fear.

If you find yourself in a season of loneliness, what can you do?

1. Remember that God is with you
2. Pray – ask God for help
3. Read God's Word – filled with encouragement, strength, hope
4. Reach out to others. This will allow you to begin taking the focus off yourself

In Psalm 25:16 we find King David asking God not only for emotional compassion but for action. He wanted God to do something; turn to me, look at me, give attention to me and be gracious—have mercy, take pity, be kind to me.

Loneliness is a pain like no other pain. My sister and I sat holding our mother's hands as she dropped her earthly rags and put on her royal robes in heaven. At that moment, we looked at each other and simultaneously spoke, "We are orphans!" Although we were together, each of us had an immediate sense of loneliness. But in those moments, God reminded us that He cares, Jesus understands, and He is our hope in the face of loneliness.

If you are struggling with loneliness, it is my prayer that you will begin to look outside yourself. Reach up to God. Reach in to begin your healing. Reach out to others. Allow yourself to find hope in the face of loneliness.

Hope for Daily Living

Write Psalm 147:3. Are you willing to allow God to heal any broken area of your heart?

Read Psalm 27:10. Write it here. Have you been rejected by family or friends? How does this verse speak to you?

Psalm 23 is a declaration/affirmation of trust in the LORD. Write it here.

Read Romans 8:35, and list three things you will do for yourself or someone you know who is dealing with loneliness.

Read John 14:18. If you are dealing with loneliness, write this verse down and tape it to your bathroom mirror, your computer, stick it in your wallet, and memorize it so you will never forget.

*Heavenly Father, Search my heart and reveal the
cracks and crevices where loneliness might settle in.
Show me if there is unforgiveness, resentment, fear,
dread, or any other traumatizing emotion lurking in
the secret places of my heart. Remind me that Your
faithfulness is my shield against the enemy. LORD, I
make You my refuge, my dwelling place, knowing
that You will guard me, protect me, and rescue me
in time of trouble. Although I may go through
periods of loneliness, I know my hope is in You.
When I wake, when I am lonely, and when it is my
time to die, remind me I am not alone. In the most
precious Name of Jesus, I pray. Amen.*

Chapter Twenty-eight

Hope

In the Midst of

Temptation

No temptation has overtaken you

but such as is common to man;

and God is faithful,

who will not allow you to be tempted

beyond what you are able,

but with the temptation

will provide the way of escape also,

so that you will be

able to endure it.

1 Corinthians 10:13 NASB

My parents often told me to be careful when choosing friends as you become like those with whom you spend a lot of time. As a child, I didn't quite get it and thought it was just an old saying passed down through the generations of my Appalachian heritage. But at age thirteen I experienced the concept and the repercussions first hand.

I had a friend who was allowed to be sassy to her mother with no fear of disciplinary action. Since she lived directly across the street, we saw each other every day. We walked to and from the school bus stop together. We climbed trees together. We walked down the street to Lake Erie and swam together. We spent a lot of time together.

I remember well the day my mother told me to do something I did not want to do. I snapped back at her with an attitude that mirrored that of my good friend. My major miscalculation—daddy overheard! That was the last spanking I ever received. You see, we were never allowed to disrespect mother in our home—under any circumstances! But I succumbed to the temptation.

1 Corinthians 10:13 explains there is no such thing as a new temptation. Wrong desires and temptations happen to everyone. The author of Psalm 91

reminds us that the LORD will save us from the fowler's snare. Like a hunter who baits a snare in order to catch a wild animal, our enemy sets a trap for us with temptations he hopes we cannot resist. The Greek word for tempted translated here into English means *to try to trap*. Satan sets a trap hoping that we will fail and sin. His motivation is to destroy; "The thief comes only to steal and kill and destroy..." (John 10:10)

When facing temptation, you may recall past failures, perhaps separation from loved ones, disappointment in yourself, or fear of repeating past behavior. But God has already prepared your way of escape, your way out, your exit from the time of temptation so you will be able to endure it, stand up under it, and bear up under it.

As recorded in Matthew 4, Jesus himself was tempted by satan. When He was hungry, satan offered Him a stone turned to bread. Standing on the highest point of the temple, satan tempted Him to prove He was God. Atop a high mountain, looking out over the kingdoms of the world, satan tempted Jesus to bow down and worship the evil one, and then he would give Jesus the world. But each time Christ answered, "It is written..."

So you see, being tempted does not mean you have

already sinned but rather the enemy is trying to get you to sin. Your way of escape, endurance, bearing up under the temptation is the Word of God. John 1 tells us the Word was in the beginning, with God, and the Word was God. "Through Him all things were made; without him nothing was made that has been made.' (John 1:3)

How do you escape temptation? You go to the Word! Hebrews 4:12-13 is a reminder that God's Word is alive, active in our lives, judging the thoughts and attitudes of our hearts. "Nothing in all creation is hidden from God's sight." Verse 13.

So, trusting the Word of God is your hope in the midst of temptation. "He will cover you with his feathers, and under his wings you will find refuge; his faithfulness will be your shield and rampart." Psalm 91:4.

Hope for Daily Living

List the top five areas in which you have been tempted recently. (Example: Anxiety)

List a Scripture that gives help and support for each of those five areas of temptation.

On a separate sheet of paper or 3 x 5 card, write out those Scriptures and post them where you will see them daily.

Write Psalm 90:12 here.

Read Psalm 91:14-16. How does that apply to your life during times of temptation?

Write Psalm 139:7-12.

Heavenly Father, I am reminded that You alone are my way of escape from all temptation. When I am tempted, help me take my eyes off myself and immediately turn them towards You and Your Word. Remind me that I am never out of Your sight. I cannot hide from You. I cannot run from You, and I cannot outsmart my tempter. I need You to rescue me, sometimes even from myself, when standing eyeball to eyeball with temptation. Remind me "Thy Word is a lamp unto my feet and a light unto my path." (Psalm 119:105) I ask in Jesus most precious Name. Amen and Amen

Chapter Twenty-nine

Hope

Renews My Strength

But those who

hope in the LORD

will renew their strength.

They will soar on wings like eagles;

they will run and not grow weary,

they will walk and not be faint.

Isaiah 40:31

Hope encompasses most areas of life. Some days we simply hope the car will start, the check will come, or no one will buy the empty lot next door. On other days, we come across situations which cause us to urgently hope. A friend and I once came across a man clinging to life in our church parking lot. While she rushed inside to call 911, I stayed with him, my hand on his sweat-drenched back, praying and hoping the EMT's would come quickly.

The EMT's arrived, but only after Art's heart stopped twice were they able to stabilize him and get him to the hospital. Over the years, that incident has reminded me of how important it is to allow my human weakness to be exchanged for God's strength by placing my hope in Him.

Trusting in God and looking expectantly to Him "gives strength to the weary and increases the power of the weak." (Isaiah 40:29) On that day, and in that circumstance, my hope in Him exchanged my weakness for His strength, His power, His might, His ability to accomplish the task before me; saving Art Weir.

Isaiah 40:31 states that hope in the LORD not only renews your strength, but allows you to "soar on wings like eagles." Science tells us that Eagles have the ability to use the winds, even strong winds, and *updrafts* from the hills and mountains to help them gain altitude—allowing them to fly long distances while saving valuable energy. Hope in God acts in the same way for you and me. By waiting for, looking for, or expecting God to accomplish what is best for you, you can rise above the fray knowing He is your strength.

So the next time you are weary from running the race of life, or you have grown tired, exhausted, fainthearted from walking through the storms of life, remember the words of Hebrews 4:16, "Let us then approach the throne of grace with confidence, so that we may receive mercy and find grace to help us in our time of need."

Hope in the LORD. Allow Him to renew your strength. Walk, run, and soar through the storms of life as He exchanges your weakness for His strength.

Hope for Daily Living

Do you believe God loves you? Do you believe God wants the best for you? Are you willing to allow Him to exchange your weakness for His strength? Write Isaiah 40:31.

The King James Bible translates this verse, "But they that wait upon the LORD..." What does it mean to you to "wait upon the LORD?"

Read Psalm 103. Write verse five.

Are you struggling with waiting on the LORD or hoping in the LORD in some area of your life? If so, write it here. Then, make two lists: the pros of hoping in the LORD on one list, and the cons of hoping in the LORD on the second list.

Now decide. To wait or not to wait. To hope or not to hope. That is the question.

Heavenly Father, Thank you for reminding me— my hope is in You. As I approach Your throne of grace with confidence, thank you for reminding me that You are my strength for the journey, my hope in the storm, my focus during trials and my assurance of renewal as I grow weary from the pilgrimage. LORD, give me the strength, Your strength, which will cause me to soar today. In Jesus Precious Name, Amen and Amen.

Chapter Thirty

Hope

In Christs' Return

While we

wait

for the blessed hope—

the glorious appearing

of our great

God and Savior,

Jesus Christ...

Titus 2:13

More than fifty years ago, preparing for wedding bells and looking forward to life with my husband occupied most of my thoughts. I waited for the day we would walk down the aisle and say, "I do!" Bridal showers, dress fittings, invitations, caterers, music, flowers, and wedding cake engaged me both emotionally and physically. And while friends and family flocked to my side to assist in preparation, the one thing I longed for was to walk down the aisle, a bride, and be with my groom.

During the Vietnam War era, separated for thirteen months as he served our nation in South Korea, we had no internet; social media, email, or skype. We had no telephone communication. Letters found their way back and forth across 6500 miles of land and sea as I yearned to hear his voice and for the day he would return. The longer he was gone, the greater my longing. A half century later, I continue to look forward to seeing him pull in the driveway and walk up the steps. I wait for his kiss and question, "Did you have a good day?"

Perhaps you too have experienced waiting to see someone and longing to be in his/her presence. Over the years, I have noticed a similarity between my thirteen-month wait for my husband's return, and my growing anticipation for the return of my Savior. Do you feel it? Some days I look toward the heavens and wait in anticipation as my heart cries out, "It is time, Lord!" How strange to look forward to the return of the One my physical eyes have not yet seen.

So for now, as the Bride of Christ longing for the return of the Bridegroom, we must wait for the glorious appearing of Jesus Christ. And while we wait, anticipate, look forward to His return, we have things to do. Wait is a verb—it shows action. Waiting for Christs' return does not indicate we should sit and do nothing. While you linger here, you are called to serve, attend to, and minister to the needs of those whom our Lord places along your journey. I must do the same. Mark 10:45 tells us why, "For even the Son of Man did not come to be served, but to serve, and to give his life as a ransom for many."

The Apostle Paul's letter to Titus repeatedly emphasizes "loving and doing and teaching what is good." (NIV Study Bible Intro to Titus) I would stress that, as the Bride of Christ, we can do no less "While we wait for the blessed hope—the glorious appearing of our great God and Savior, Jesus Christ."

So let us keep our Wedding Garments clean and remember the words of the Apostle Paul to

Timothy, "Now there is in store for me the crown of righteousness, which the Lord, the righteous Judge, will award to me on that day—and not only to me, but also to all who have longed for his appearing." (2 Timothy 4:8) And then we will feast as we sit down at the Wedding Supper, "...Blessed are those who are invited to the Wedding Supper of the Lamb." (Revelation 19:9)

Hope for Daily Living

Do you live in excited expectation for the return of Christ? Why or why not?

Read Titus chapter two. How can you apply Paul's exhortation to Titus in your life? Make a list.

Read Revelation 19:5-9. Write verses 7-9.

Do you know, understand, and believe that you will be seated at the Wedding Supper with Christ? If you are not certain, please prayerfully read the Scriptures found on page 223. It would also be wise to speak with your pastor and/or the pastor of a Bible believing/teaching church.

If you have already received Christ as Savior, and/or you have never written down your testimony, write it here. This will enable you to be prepared to share it with others. "But in your hearts set apart Christ as Lord. Always be prepared to give an answer to everyone who asks you to give the reason for the hope that you have. But do this with gentleness and respect." (1 Peter 3: 15)

Heavenly Father, as I anxiously await the glorious appearing of our great God and Savior, Jesus Christ, I am excited to live life in the here and now, serving You and ministering in the Name of Jesus. Help me to walk in love, humility, and peace among my fellow man. Make me aware of those around me who do not know Christ. Give me the wisdom and courage to "fear not" in the face of anxiety and uncertainty. May I stand strong for You in the face of adversity. Help me temper my speech with the fruit of the Spirit. Help me to be bold when the situation calls for boldness and meek when the situation calls for quiet strength. Above all, help me to always be willing to stand firm for the gospel of Jesus Christ—no matter the consequences. While I wait, help me be an effective witness to those who do not know Christ.

"He who testified to these things says, "Yes, I am coming soon." Amen. Come Lord Jesus. The grace of the Lord Jesus be with God's people. Amen." (Revelation 22:20-21)

Chapter Thirty-one

Our Hope is the

Power In the

Blood

of Jesus

For this is my blood
of the covenant,
which is poured out
for many for the
forgiveness
of
sins.

Matthew 26:28

A person can live only a few days without water.
Without food one can survive several weeks—
without oxygen only a few minutes. Without blood
life ends! Blood supplies the means of travel for
every necessary component to keep our bodies
functioning properly. Medical research indicates
that approximately three hundred billion red cells
die and are replaced every day—the new strong
clean blood replaces the toxic day after day, year
after year throughout our life. There is power in the
blood.

Life is in the blood. The Jews understood and today
practicing Jews continue to eat only kosher meat
from an animal that has had its blood drained in
preparation for cooking. Imagine the surprise and
perhaps horror of the Jewish followers of Christ
when he announced "Truly, truly, I say to you,
unless you eat the flesh of the Son of Man and drink
his blood, you have no life in you." (John 6:53 ESV)

Christ was teaching the truth of the spiritual life by
teaching the truth of the physical life. He came to
die, to shed His blood for the redemption of
mankind—you and me. After His death on the
Cross of Calvary, it would no longer be necessary to
shed the blood of goats and bulls as a sacrifice to
atone for the sins of man. Christ came to be the
ultimate sacrifice.

Christ's blood has the power to cleanse us from our
sin! Like me, you have probably heard this phrase:
The red blood (of Christ) washes away my black

sin and makes me white as snow. How is that possible? There is power in the blood of Christ! Just as the blood in our bodies cleanses toxins such as carbon dioxide from our bodies, the blood of Christ cleanses us from sin's toxin.

Our physical blood sustains our physical life. The blood of Christ, the purchase price for our eternal life, washes and sustains our life in Christ. Through His blood we are free from the burden of sin, the grasp of satan, the guilt and condemnation that encompassed life before Christ. It is not necessary, nor are we able to "clean up" before coming to Christ. As we accept Christ as Savior, His cleansing blood cleans us and transforms our life of sin washing away the toxins and replacing them with the power of Almighty God to live life in Christ Jesus.

John 3:16 tells us that, "For God so loved the world, that he gave his only Son, that whoever believes in him should not perish but have eternal life." (ESV) In the blood of Christ there is hope, there is salvation, there is LIFE eternal! There is power in the blood of Christ, and it is available to whoever believes. **Will you believe?**

The Problem of Sin

Romans 3:23— "For all have sinned and fall short of the glory of God…"

The Wages of Sin

Romans 6:23a—"For the wages of sin is death…"

The Love of God

Romans 5:8—"But God demonstrates His own love toward us, in that while we were still sinners, Christ died for us."

The Free Gift of Salvation

Romans 6:23b—"But the gift of God is eternal life in Christ Jesus our Lord."

Accepting the Free Gift

Romans 10:9 & 13—"That if you confess with your mouth the Lord Jesus and believe in your heart that God has raised Him from the dead, you will be saved. (13) For whoever calls on the name of the LORD shall be saved."

Precious Friend,

God is offering you new life in Jesus Christ. Would you accept His gift of eternal life today?

Through prayer to God with a sincere repentant heart:

1. Admit you are a sinner, ask God for forgiveness, and turn from your sin.
2. Confess that Jesus, the Son of God, died on the cross and rose again to save you from your sin.
3. Invite Jesus to be the Savior and Lord of your life. (Accept Jesus Christ's payment for your sins. Choose to follow Jesus as your Lord.)

If you don't know what to say, you can pray something similar to this:

Dear God, I know that I am a sinner. I am asking for Your forgiveness, and I want to turn away from my sins. I believe that Jesus Christ, Your Son, died on the cross and rose again to save me from my sins, and I now put my faith and trust in Him as my personal Lord and Savior. Amen.

If you have prayed from a sincere heart to receive Christ, you **are** forgiven and included in the Family—a Child of God. As a follower of Christ, you will want to connect with a Bible-believing church to grow in your faith and serve God with other Christians. Don't delay—tell someone you know about your decision to follow Jesus Christ, and talk with a Pastor or Christian friend about how to learn more about our Lord and the Christian life.

Congratulations, and welcome to the family!

"Whoever calls upon the name of

The Lord shall be saved."

—Romans 10:13

If you have recently accepted Christ as Savior or renewed your commitment to follow Christ, I would like to hear from you in order to add your name to my prayer list.

You may contact me at:

roadsignsforliving@gmail.com
roadsignsforliving.blogspot.com
Facebook.com/Joyce Powell Author

In His Grace,
Joyce Powell

Other books available from Joyce L Powell are *Reflections*, *Grace for Living*, and *RoadSigns for Living*, and can be purchased from amazon.com or by contacting Joyce via roadsignsforliving@gmail.com or at http://www.roadsignsforliving.blogspot.com.

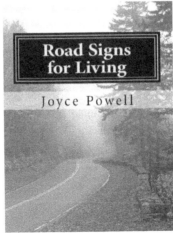

ABOUT THE AUTHOR

Joyce Powell was born in Kentucky but early in life her family moved to Michigan where she grew, graduated from high school and met and married her husband of fifty years. She attended LMU in Harrogate, TN and TWU in Denton, TX.

She and her husband have a daughter, two sons and nine grandchildren. In 2003, they moved to the Texas Hill Country to enjoy family. She has organized and taught songwriting seminars, women's Bible studies, and has been involved in singing and playing piano for various Gospel groups since the age of sixteen. She has participated in ministry in Texas maximum security prisons, including men's death row.

A member of the Women's Ministry Team at her church; she speaks at women's retreats and conferences as well as teaching Women's Bible Studies.

Her first book, a devotional—"Reflections: God's Love, Mercy, and Grace" was published in December 2013. Her second devotional, "Grace for Living," came in 2014 and her first published Bible Study "Road Signs for Living," an inter-active study for women, became a reality in February, 2015. "Words of Hope—Help for the Hurting Heart" is expected to be released by September 30, 2016.

While she also enjoys combining her landscape and nature photography with words of inspiration and encouragement on large prints and greeting cards, her heart's cry is to spread the Word of God and the message of salvation while reaching out to the broken.